War Crimes in the Balkans

Medicine Under Siege
in the former Yugoslavia
1991-1995

Physicians for Human Rights

Physicians for Human Rights
Boston • San Francisco • Chicago

Library of Congress Catalog Card No. 96-067670
ISBN: 1-879707-20-9

Cover design: Glenn Ruga/Visual Communications

Cover photo: Glenn Ruga

Graveyard in front of home in Hrasnica, a suburb of Sarajevo, 1995.

PHYSICIANS FOR HUMAN RIGHTS

Physicians for Human Rights (PHR) is an organization of health professionals, scientists, and concerned citizens which uses the knowledge and skills of the medical and forensic sciences to investigate and prevent violations of international human rights and humanitarian law.

Since 1986, PHR members have worked to stop torture, disappearances, and political killings by governments and opposition groups; to improve health and sanitary conditions in prisons and detention centers; to investigate the physical and psychological consequences of violations of humanitarian law in internal and international conflicts; to defend medical neutrality and the right of civilians and combatants to receive medical care during times of war; to protect health professionals who are victims of violations of human rights; and to prevent medical complicity in torture and other abuses.

PHR conducts educational and training projects for health professionals, members of the judiciary, and human rights advocates on the application of medical and forensic skills in the investigation of violations of human rights. PHR bases its actions on the Universal Declaration of Human Rights and other international human rights and humanitarian agreements. The organization adheres to a policy of strict impartiality and is concerned with the medical consequences of human rights abuses regardless of the ideology of the offending government or group.

Charles Clements, M.D., is President; Carola Eisenberg, M.D., is Vice President; Leonard S. Rubenstein is Executive Director; Susannah Sirkin is Deputy Director; Charlotte McCormick is Director of Finance and Administration; Kari Hannibal is Membership and Education Coordinator; Barbara Ayotte is Senior Program Associate; Vincent Iacopino, M.D., is Western Regional Director; Robert H. Kirschner, M.D., is director of the International Forensic Program, and Eric Stover is Senior Consultant.

Physicians for Human Rights
100 Boylston Street, Suite 702
Boston, MA 02116 USA
Tel. (617) 695-0041/Fax. (617) 695-0307
email: phrusa@igc.apc.org

"The blood massacre in Bangladesh quickly covered the memory of the Russian invasion of Czechoslovakia; the assassination of Allende drowned out the groans of Bangladesh; the war in the Sinai desert made people forget Allende; the Cambodian massacre made people forget Sinai; and so on and so forth, until everyone lets everything be forgotten."

Milan Kundera
The Book of Laughter and
Forgetting

"The wrongs which we seek to condemn and punish have been so calculated, so malignant and so devastating, that civilization cannot tolerate their being ignored, because it cannot survive their being repeated."

Justice Robert Jackson
Chief Prosecutor,
Nuremburg War Crime
Trials

CONTENTS

PREFACE

For several years, we have seen reports on the evening television news of shelling of hospitals across the former Yugoslavia. From the comfort of our homes, we repeatedly watched health workers dodge snipers or mortar fire as they attempted to rescue wounded civilians in Sarajevo and other cities. We read in our morning newspapers of the shelling and blocking and, in some cases, looting, of relief convoys carrying medical supplies.

International law provides that civilian and military leaders who wage war must consider medical personnel and their facilities and vehicles neutral and thus immune from attack. Similarly, physicians and nurses who attend to the victims of war must perform their professional duties without discrimination and uphold the fundamental precept of medical ethics *primum non nocere*--above all do no harm.

As long as human beings have waged war, there have been attempts to temper its consequences. In the fifteenth and sixteenth centuries, at a time when there were virtually no limits to the barbarity of warfare, there was one unwritten law that all sides abided to: the water wells must not be poisoned. Even then there was an understanding that all sides in a conflict had to protect and limit the damage to structures necessary for the survival of civilian populations. Five hundred years later, that same understanding guides our rights and responsibilities as health professionals to ensure the health and survival of affected populations during times of conflict.

In World War I, civilian casualties accounted for no more than five percent of all deaths. But, in World War II, that figure climbed to fifty percent. In recent decades, civilian casualties have accounted for as many as eighty or ninety percent of all deaths in war. The principles enshrined in international law to protect civilians in times of war seem to have been unraveling in the latter half of the twentieth century.

ix

By convening an International Criminal Tribunal with the responsibility to investigate and prosecute war crimes, crimes against humanity, and genocide in the former Yugoslavia, the United Nations has, in effect, said that the world community can no longer ignore the enforcement of international and humanitarian law. We at PHR feel this is a historic opportunity that promises justice for victims and their families, deterrence against further abuse, and an essential part of the basis for eventual peace and reconciliation. It is only through individual accountability rather than collective condemnation that we can hope to diffuse the ethnic violence that has characterized the conflicts of the region.

In November 1995, the International Criminal Tribunal indicted three high-ranking Serbian officers of the Yugoslav Peoples' Army for war crimes committed in the Croatian town of Ovcara, near Vukovar. Soldiers under the command of these officers had led 155 male prisoners from a hospital in Vukovar, executed them at an abandoned farm in Ovcara, and buried evidence of their crime in a mass grave. Medical and forensic evidence-- unearthed from this grave a year later by Physicians for Human Rights --led to the indictments.

This report presents evidence of such "violations of medical neutrality" committed by the warring factions in the former Yugoslavia since 1991. The report's findings are based upon several PHR medical and forensic missions to the region. Evidence from several of these missions has been presented to the International Criminal Tribunal.

As health professionals, we have a responsibility to insure that the laws of war remain bulwarks against the behavior they seek to discourage rather than historical artifacts of idealists. Since the beginning of the conflict in the former Yugoslavia there have been courageous efforts by both health workers and human rights activists to focus attention on violations of the laws of war.

Our professional societies and associations, such as the World Medical Association, the World Council of Nurses, and the many national affiliates which give them legitimacy, neglected the citizens of the former Yugoslavia when they failed to speak out against atrocities. Health professionals from throughout the region have complained, often bitterly, to PHR representatives about their sense of abandonment by their foreign colleagues.

We urge you not only to read this report, but to use it. Whether reading this report leads to classroom sessions, discussions amongst colleagues or resolutions within professional societies, education of policy makers is largely dependent on what we as health professionals choose to do with the knowledge that we have gained. It is our hope that this information can be used to help us develop better strategies to protect the sick and wounded, as well as those who care for them, in future conflicts.

Above all, it can help to insure that the "forgetting" Milan Kundera refers to in the quote on the coverleaf does not happen yet again. We owe this to our colleagues in the former Yugoslavia and elsewhere, who have too often felt abandoned and whose voices need to be heard.

Charles Clements, M.D.
President

GLOSSARY OF ACRONYMS

HVO	Croatian Defense Council
ICRC	International Committee of the Red Cross
ICN	International Council of Nurses
IFOR	Implementation Force
IPTF	International Police Task Force
JNA	Yugoslav Peoples' Army
NATO	North Atlantic Treaty Organization
PHR	Physicians for Human Rights
UN	United Nations
UNESCO	United Nations Educational, Scientific and Cultural Organization
UNHCR	United Nations High Commissioner for Refugees
UNICEF	United Nations Children's Fund
UNPROFOR	United Nations Protection Force
WHO	World Health Organization
WMA	World Medical Association

ACKNOWLEDGMENTS

This report was written by Eric Stover, former Executive Director and currently Senior Consultant of Physicians for Human Rights (PHR) and Richard P. Claude, a PHR consultant and Professor Emeritus, University of Maryland, College Park and Visiting Professor, Princeton University. The report was edited by Ana Carrigan; Barbara Ayotte, Senior Program Associate of Physicians for Human Rights; and Susannah Sirkin, Deputy Director of Physicians for Human Rights. It was prepared for production by Ayotte and Laura Reiner, Program Associate, Physicians for Human Rights.

The report is based on research conducted by PHR in the former Yugoslavia between October 1992 and November 1995. It includes information received from the UN Commission of Experts which investigated grave breaches of international humanitarian law committed in the former federation since 1991.

PHR is greatly indebted to many people and institutions in Bosnia, Croatia, and Serbia for their help in preparing this report who requested that their names not be listed for security purposes.

We wish to thank Human Rights Watch/Helsinki and the following persons for their assistance in preparing this report: James Welsh; Marsha Campbell; H. Jack Geiger, M.D., Charles Clements, M.D., Mary E. Black, M.D.; Jill Guzman; Nicholas Evageliou; Cherif Bassiouni; William Schiller; Douglas W. Cassel, Jr.; Jemera Rone; Levi Roque, M.D.; Allen Keller, M.D.; Maricela Daniel; Michael O'Flaherty; Ivana Nizich; Tom Osorio; Tony Garcia; Harold Siam, M.D.; Paul Norton; Marco Sassoli; Hernan Reyes, M.D.; Jane Schaller, M.D.; Thomas Crane, M.D; Aryeh Neier, and Diane Paul.

PHR expresses its appreciation to the Soros/Open Society Fund, the Rockefeller Foundation, the Smith-Richardson Foundation, the New Land Foundation, and the John Merck Fund for their support of our work in the former Yugoslavia. We also thank the following corporations for their donations of vital equipment used during our investigations: Miles Dental Products (dental X-ray film), Henry Schein Co. (dental X-ray equipment), Baxter Health Care Hospital Supply (surgical supplies), Shandon Lipshaw (autopsy equipment), GE Medical Systems (X-ray and fluoroscopy machines), Sokkia Corporation (surveying equipment), Polaroid Corporation (Spectra cameras and film), AGFA Corporation, Matrix Division (X-ray processors and accessory equipment), AGFA Compu Graphic (film), Lufthansa (airline tickets), Kamp Air Freight (shipping).

I. INTRODUCTION

No one of conscience can ignore the moral dimension of the Yugoslav crisis. Since the summer of 1991, when war broke out in Slovenia and Croatia, tens--and possibly hundreds--of thousands of people have been killed. Rape and torture have been turned into weapons of war and used to terrorize communities. Hundreds of thousands of people have been deported or forced to flee their homes. The region now holds over 2.7 million refugees and internally displaced persons. And there is evidence of over 150 mass graves of civilians who were summarily executed by military and paramilitary forces.[1]

Tens of thousands of NATO troops have arrived in Bosnia-Herzegovina to enforce a peace accord brokered in December 1995 at the Wright-Patterson Air Force Base in Dayton, Ohio. At the same time, the International Criminal Tribunal for the former Yugoslavia ("International Criminal Tribunal") has announced the indictments of fifty-seven individuals, including charges of genocide against Bosnian Serb leader Radovan Karadžić and the head of the Bosnian Serb military, Ratko Mladić.[2]

Physicians for Human Rights (PHR) has been monitoring human rights abuses in the wars in the former Yugoslavia since 1992.[3] In October 1992, PHR sent a research mission to the

---

[1] See *Final Report of the Commission of Experts Established Pursuant to Security Council Resolution 780 (1992)*, S/1994/674, 27 May 1994 and Annexes, S/1994/674/Add. 2 (Vol. I-V), December 28, 1994.

[2] Indictments, United Nations International Criminal Tribunal for the former Yugoslavia, IT/95/5/D337-D315, July 24, 1995.

[3] Participants in the eight PHR missions to the former Yugoslavia were: (1) October 12-26, 1992: H. Jack Geiger, M.D. and Clyde Snow, Ph.D.; (2) December 17-19, 1992: Eric Stover, Clyde

former federation to investigate war-related trauma among refugees. The team also collected evidence of mass killings of civilians. Seven other PHR missions have followed to document violations of medical neutrality, assess reports of widespread rape, and carry out exhumations of mass graves. Many of these missions have gathered physical evidence of war crimes for the International Criminal Tribunal.

Evidence collected by a PHR team in November 1992 from a mass grave at Vukovar, Croatia contributed to indictments issued in November 1995 by the International Criminal Tribunal. Three senior officers of the Yugoslav Peoples' Army (JNA) were allegedly responsible "for the mass killing at Ovčara, near Vukovar (Eastern Slavonia region of Croatia), of approximately 260 captive non-Serb men who had been removed from the Vukovar Hospital on November 20, 1991."[4]

Snow, Ph.D., Rebecca Ann Saunders, Ph.D., and Morris Tidball-Binz, M.D.; (3) January 23-February 6, 1993: H. Jack Geiger, M.D., Mary E. Black, M.D., Thomas Crane, M.D., John Woodall, M.D., Jeffrey Sonis, M.D., and Nancy Sugg, M.D.; (4) January 12-23, 1993: Shana Swiss, M.D.; (5) March 8-23, 1993: Eric Stover and Clyde Snow, Ph.D.; (6) October 15-November 15, 1993: Eric Stover, Clyde Snow, Ph.D., Robert H. Kirschner, M.D., William Haglund, Ph.D., Douglas Scott, Ph.D., Luis Fondebrider, Stefan Schmitt, Melissa Connor, Ph.D., Francis Calabrese, Ph.D., Ralph Hartley, Ph.D., Burney McClurkan, Mercedes Doretti, Ivan Caceres, and Isabel Reveco; (7) October 2-11, 1995: Eric Stover, William Haglund, Ph.D., and Andrew Thomson, M.D.; (8) November 4-17, 1995: Eric Stover, Clyde Snow, Ph.D., Robert H. Kirschner, M.D., Stefan Schmitt, William Haglund, Ph.D., and Peter S. Vanezis, M.D.

[4] United Nations International Criminal Tribunal for the former Yugoslavia, "Three JNA Officers from a Belgrade-Based Brigade Charged with the Mass Killing of Non-Serb Men Forcibly Removed from the Vukovar Hospital," press release, The Hague, November 9, 1995.

This report examines the wars in the former Yugoslavia through the prism of medical neutrality. Medical neutrality[5] is a principle enshrined in medical ethics and international humanitarian and human rights law that seeks to limit injury and death to civilians and combatants who are *hors de combat* (prisoners of war) during times of war. Under international law, medical personnel must uphold medical ethics,[6] respect patient confidentiality, and treat all sick and wounded without regard to their belligerent status, ethnicity, or religious and political views.

Since its founding in 1986, PHR has sought to promote the principle of medical neutrality and the rights of civilians and combatants to receive medical care, whether the conflict was

---

[5] It is important to emphasize that "medical neutrality" is not a field of international law; it is a normative construct which draws on international humanitarian and human rights law, in combination with medical ethics, to provide standards for health professionals with respect to their rights and duties under various circumstances of war and peace. However, abuses which fall under the rubric of violations of medical neutrality can, in themselves, constitute grave breaches of international humanitarian law. (See Table 2: Classification of Violations of Medical Neutrality, p. 66)

[6] The ethical responsibilities of physicians and other health professionals are the same in war and peace. For instance, Article 1 of the "Declaration of Tokyo," adopted by the World Medical Association (WMA) in 1975, states:

> The doctor shall not countenance, condone or participate in the practice of torture or other forms of cruel, inhuman or degrading procedures, whatever the offense of which the victim of such procedures is suspected, accused, or guilty, and whatever the victim's beliefs or motives, and in all situations, including armed conflict and civil strife.

international, as in the former Yugoslavia,[7] or non-international, as in El Salvador or Mexico.[8] As an organization of health professionals, scientists, and concerned citizens, PHR has been concerned not only for the safety of its medical colleagues but for the thousands of actual or potential patients who could suffer because they are denied medical services.

Sources of Information

PHR gathered information for this report from several sources. Forensic experts collected medicolegal evidence from mass graves. They also interviewed witnesses and reviewed postmortem and crime scene photographs. PHR physicians interviewed, and in some cases, medically examined, victims of torture and other forms of abuse in Croatia, Serbia, and Bosnia-Herzegovina. PHR representatives also interviewed dozens of health professionals in clinics, hospitals, and medical schools throughout the countries of the former Yugoslavia and in the United States and Europe. Information was also obtained from personnel serving with the United Nations and with non-governmental organizations providing relief assistance in the former Yugoslavia, and public health officials with international, national, and local organizations.

---

[7] The Yugoslav conflict started as an internal conflict but became international in character after international recognition of the independence of Slovenia and Croatia in 1991.

[8] See Physicians for Human Rights, *El Salvador: Health Care Under Siege: Violations of Medical Neutrality During the Civil Conflict,* (Boston: Physicians for Human Rights, 1990) and Physicians for Human Rights and Human Rights Watch/Americas, *Waiting for Justice in Chiapas* (Boston: Physicians for Human Rights, 1994). See also, L. Magarrell, "Violations of Medical Neutrality in El Salvador," in G.L. Wackers and C.T.M. Wennekes (eds.), *Violations of Medical Neutrality,* (Amsterdam: Thesis Press, 1992), pp. 55-71.

Many of those interviewed by PHR have asked that their names be kept confidential, and some, that the place of the interview remain secret, because it might help identify them. Many people fear for the lives of friends and relatives who remain in the war zone, or that their enemies might find them in refugee camps and other placement centers, even when these areas are far removed from the war zone or are no longer active war zones. In deference to their concerns, PHR has avoided identifying certain sources.

PHR has supplemented its interviews with information obtained from Human Rights Watch/Helsinki and from the files of the UN Commission of Experts to Investigate Grave Breaches of International Humanitarian Law in the former Yugoslavia since 1991 ("Commission of Experts").

PHR is concerned that the scope and brutality of abuses in the former Yugoslavia far exceed those reported here. This report does not attempt to document every violation of medical neutrality committed in the former Yugoslavia since 1991. Instead, it examines the ways in which "ethnic cleansing" and other abuses have affected the normal functioning of hospitals and clinics and the delivery of medical care throughout the former federation.

Summary of Conclusions and Recommendations

Since the outbreak of war in the former Yugoslavia in 1991, both massive human rights abuses and flagrant disregard for medical neutrality have been widespread throughout the region. All sides in the conflict have blatantly disregarded the rule of proportionality, which holds that civilian casualties and damage to civilian objects should not be out of proportion to the military advantages anticipated. Hospitals and clinics in or near conflict zones have been deliberately and often repeatedly attacked. Patients and medical staff have been shot by snipers and, in at least one case, forcibly removed from hospital wards and summarily executed. Ambulances and other medical vehicles have been the target of mortar and sniper fire. Relief convoys carrying medical supplies have been shelled or prevented from reaching towns and cities under siege. In some instances, the warring factions, particularly the Bosnian Serbs, have obstructed the delivery of humanitarian aid to civilians, or have allowed relief supplies to pass through check points, only after they have confiscated a percentage of foods and medicines. Bosnian Serb forces have blockaded the delivery of relief aid in an effort to starve, and thereby force, the besieged population to flee or surrender. None of these actions has served a purpose other than to terrorize the civilian population and destroy its infrastructure.

The findings in this report, and reports by other human rights organizations[9] and independent news media, provide evidence that war crimes and acts of genocide have been committed in Bosnia-Herzegovina. Since July 1994, indictments have been issued against 57 individuals--43 Bosnian Serbs, 8 Croats, 3 Serbian JNA officers, and 3 Bosnian Muslims.[10] In July 1995, the International Criminal Tribunal charged Radovan Karadžić, M.D., a psychiatrist and the political leader of the Bosnian Serbs, and General Ratko Mladić, the commander of the Bosnian Serb army, with several crimes including acts of genocide. The International Criminal Tribunal found that the two men were responsible for "ethnic cleansing" campaigns directed against Muslims and Croats on the basis of their religion and ethnicity. The victims of these campaigns have been expelled from their homes and villages; rounded up and held in detention

---

[9] Detailed and extensive documentation of massive human rights abuses in Bosnia-Herzegovina can be found in two Helsinki Watch reports: *War Crimes in Bosnia-Herzegovina* and *War Crimes in Bosnia-Herzegovina (Volume II)*, published by Human Rights Watch. Copies of the reports can be obtained by writing Human Rights Watch, 485 Fifth Avenue, New York, NY 10017-6104.

[10] Bulletin of the International Criminal Tribunal for the former Yugoslavia, January 1996 and C. Hedges, "Balkan War Crimes: Bosnia is First to Turn in Its Own," *The New York Times*, May 3, 1996, p.3.

camps; raped and tortured; deported; killed in indiscriminate attacks; and summarily executed.

Recommendations

1. Cooperation with and Support of the International Criminal Tribunal

• Physicians for Human Rights believes that the creation of the International Criminal Tribunal is an historic opportunity to demonstrate that genocide, war crimes, and crimes against humanity cannot be committed with impunity. By establishing individual guilt, trials such as those promised by the International Criminal Tribunal will help dispel the notion of collective blame for these crimes. Moreover, PHR does not believe a peace will ever last in the former Yugoslavia unless respect for international law and justice are made integral to the implementation of the peace agreement. To this end, the United Nations and individual governments should increase their financial and diplomatic support of the International Criminal Tribunal.

• Physicians for Human Rights calls on the parties to the conflict in the former Yugoslavia to discipline or punish those responsible for violations of human rights and humanitarian law, including violations of medical neutrality.

• The lifting of sanctions against the Serbian government should be strictly linked to full cooperation with the investigation and extradition of suspected war criminals; release of all prisoners; the closing of all forced labor camps; the assuring of the right to return for displaced civilians, as well as the right to remain; and access to humanitarian and human rights groups.

• The major powers, and particularly the U.S. government, should disclose all available information, including intelligence reports, of atrocities committed in the former Yugoslavia. The United Nations and other individual governments must insist that the International Criminal Tribunal be free to follow wherever the evidence leads.

• Given reports and other evidence that the Bosnian Serb forces may have executed thousands of Muslim men from Srebrenica and Zepa, the United Nations and individual governments should demand that the Bosnian Serbs give the International Criminal Tribunal and international humanitarian and human rights organizations immediate access to all detainees being held by Bosnian Serb forces in the region.

• The International Criminal Tribunal should have immediate access to alleged execution sites in the Srebrenica area. The NATO-led multinational Implementation Force (IFOR) and the International Civilian Police Task Force (IPTF) should provide in a timely manner the security and logistical support requested by the International Criminal Tribunal staff investigating alleged war crimes in Bosnia and Herzegovina. **This should include landmine detection and clearance, as well as round-the-clock guarding of sites selected by the International Criminal Tribunal for investigation, and security escort for the equipment needed for the scientific investigation of mass graves.**

• IFOR should use decisive military action to stop any future massacres of civilians in Bosnia and Herzegovina. No member of IFOR or other international staff should have any association with indicted war criminals other than to arrest them.

II. Protection of Medical Personnel, Facilities and Patients: Safeguarding of Medical Neutrality

• The United Nations should take measures to safeguard medical neutrality in its protection and peacekeeping mandates, including amending their provisions, developing monitoring systems, warning commanders of their obligations to protect civilian and medical facilities, issuing public condemnations and demanding prosecutions for war crimes when violations occur.

• Medical associations in the former Yugoslavia should ensure that their members strictly adhere to the ethical duties and obligations adopted by the World Medical Association in 1956 which state, in part, that the physician must give required care without discrimination. These associations must also prevent the publication in professional journals of articles that promote ethnic or religious hatred.

III. International Medical Response

• National medical associations worldwide must take a more active role in supporting colleagues who continue to practice medicine during armed conflicts. They, along with international associations such as the World Medical Association and the International Council of Nurses must develop strategies to support beleaguered colleagues and their patients, condemn publicly violations of medical neutrality when they occur, and educate civilian and military officials about the duties and responsibilities of medical personnel, and the basic legal safeguards intended to protect civilians and medical facilities in times of war. PHR urges professional associations to take a pro-active stance to protect patients and their colleagues at the onset of conflicts by developing rapid assessment and response capacities, creating "correspondence networks", and providing material support.

II. HISTORICAL AND LEGAL BACKGROUND

Early History

Slavic people moved into the Balkan peninsula in the sixth and seventh centuries A.D.[11] The Slavs in the western region (Slovenes and Croatians) came under the influence of the Roman Catholic Church, whereas Slavs in the eastern region (Serbians) adopted the Orthodox faith. Bosnians came under the influence of both.[12]

From the fourteenth through sixteenth centuries, the Turks advanced through the Balkans. The regions closer to Turkey (Serbia and Macedonia) were conquered first and liberated last, while those closer to central Europe (Croatia) were conquered last and liberated first. Serbia, for instance, was conquered in 1389 and achieved autonomous rule in 1833, while Croatia was conquered in the early 1500s but was liberated from Turkey in the late 1600s.

The ethnogenesis of the Bosnian Muslims began after the Kingdom of Bosnia (1463) and the Duchy of Herzegovina fell to the Ottoman Empire.[13] The Turkish yoke prevailed for 400

---

[11] For the purposes of this report, this brief historical review examines events in the former Yugoslavia through the lens of ethnic relations. PHR acknowledges that economics and politics have played a major role in the history of the former Yugoslavia.

[12] S. Clissold, ed., *A Short History of Yugoslavia: From Early Times to 1966* (Cambridge: Cambridge University Press, 1966), p. 11.

[13] B. Hall, *The Impossible Country: A Journey Through the Last Days of Yugoslavia* (London: Penguin Books, 1994), p. 120-121 and R. West, *Black Lamb and Grey Falcon* (New York: Penguin Books, 1940),

years, during which time "there were wholesale conversions to Islam, unlike any other area of the Ottoman Empire except Albania." [14] The acceptance of Islam by Bosnians and Slavicized immigrants has many explanations and is consistent with a tradition of shifting religions in pre-Ottoman Bosnia-Herzegovina.

During the eighteenth century, Croatia fell under the influence of Hungary and subsequently of Austria, in part to ward off the Turkish threat. The Austro-Hungarian influence spread southward and Bosnia was occupied in the late nineteenth century. This was a period notable for a marked rise in nationalism throughout the Balkans. In both Croatia and Serbia, the struggle for political independence was accelerated by strong nationalistic sentiments. The Serbs sought independence from the Turks, and the Croatians from the Austro-Hungarian Empire. At the same time, calls for the unity of all southern Slavs increased (Yugoslavia, in literal translation, means "Land of the South Slavs").

Rise of Modern Nationalism

Nationalistic impulses in the nineteenth century prompted acts of expansionism and intolerance on all sides. After Croatia annexed Slavonia (adjacent to Serbia), Serbs came to constitute twenty-five percent of the Croatian population, yet the ethnic Serbs were denied equal rights as a minority. As late as 1902, there were anti-Serb riots in Zagreb, the Croatian capital. In Bosnia, although there were no overt anti-Serb or anti-Croat activities, the Bosnian Serbs remained economically

---

pp. 299-303.

[14] R.V. Weeks, ed., *Muslim Peoples, A World Ethnographic Survey, 2nd Revised Edition* (Westport, CT: Greenwood Press, 1984), Volume 1, pp. 172-177 at 173.

disadvantaged: seventy-four percent of the serfs in Bosnia were Serb, while only forty-three percent of the population was Serb.[15]

Serbia, having driven out the Turks by 1878 and increasingly under the economic influence of the Austro-Hungarian Empire, desired the regions of Bosnia and Macedonia to gain an outlet to the sea. In the first Balkan War (1912), a Serb-Bulgarian alliance wrested Macedonia from Turkey, and in the second Balkan War (1913), Serbia obtained Macedonia from Bulgaria.

Despite the nationalistic tendencies of the individual countries, the Serb victories in the Balkan wars ignited pan-South Slavic flames throughout the region, and led to the development of the Yugoslav state shortly after World War I. The Yugoslav dream, however, soon developed into a nightmare. Both the early parliamentary government (1919-1929) and the subsequent monarchy were racked by Croatian accusations of Serbian hegemony.[16] The government founded after the death of King Alexander in 1934 was no more successful at uniting the diverse interests of the constituent states.

In World War II, relations between the ethnic groups went from bad to worse. Germany conquered Yugoslavia in less than two weeks and the Axis powers established the "Independent State of Croatia," encompassing Croatia and Bosnia-Herzegovina. This new political entity was ruled by the *Ustashe*, a group of Croat fascists who had lived in exile during the 1930s. The Ustashe carried out a murderous policy of mass extermination against Serbs and Jews. In Bosnia, some Muslims joined the Ustashe

---

[15] S. Clissold, *A Short History of Yugoslavia*, p. 71.

[16] D. Doder, *The Yugoslavs* (New York: Vintage Books, 1978), pp. 21, 203.

ranks, and participated in atrocities and terrorist acts against the
Bosnian Serbs.[17]

In Serbia, the Chetniks, a Serb nationalist group
ideologically committed to Serbian dominance in the expected
post-war Yugoslavia, developed local strength on the basis of
guerrilla activity against the Germans. The Chetniks, however,
devoted most of their energies to vengeance against their fellow
Yugoslavs, carrying out massacres against Croats and Muslims in
ethnically-mixed areas. By the end of the war, over ten percent of
the Yugoslav population had been killed, mostly as a result of
internecine warfare.[18]

Yugoslavia Under Marshal Tito

In 1945, the Partisans, a communist resistance movement
commanded by Marshal Tito and comprised of all ethnic groups,
defeated the Axis powers and assumed control of the machinery of
the state. Marshal Tito ruled from 1945 to 1980 with
unquestioned authority. To reduce ethnic animosities he adopted
the slogan, "Brotherhood and Unity," signifying ethnic harmony
through one-party rule.

Under Tito's socialist regime, a well-organized and
sophisticated national health care system was established, which
relied on a model developed by the World Health Organization.
Clinical Center Hospitals, or teaching hospitals, were at the apex
of the system. Below these tertiary care/teaching facilities were
conventional city or county hospitals. Specialty hospitals were

---

[17] J. Tomasevich, *War and Revolution in Yugoslavia, 1941-1945:*
The Chetniks (Palo Alto, CA: Stanford University Press, 1975), p. 108.

[18] In his book, *The Yugoslavs*, Dusko Doder estimates that of the
1.7 million Yugoslavs killed in World War II, over eighty-two percent
were civilians killed by fellow Yugoslavs.

also established for specific conditions such as children's illnesses, tuberculosis, or mental health problems. At the lowest tier were small clinics, staffed by doctors and nurses who treated common ailments. Yugoslav health professionals could rightly take pride in their well-organized health care system, which was comparable to most western European countries. Under Tito, the Yugoslav health system met the country's health needs thus serving to bolster his integrationist aspirations, which were dependent on the state's attention to social needs.[19]

Although Tito's power was unchallenged, many Croats resented that most of the positions in the central government were in the hands of Serbs. Many Serbs, meanwhile, believed that Tito, a Croat by birth, was weakening Serbia through his administrative actions. In the immediate post-war period, Tito made large-scale transfers of industry to Croatia and Bosnia.[20]

After Tito's death in May 1980, Yugoslavia was governed by a rotation of the leadership among the constituent republics. Now, nationalist currents, quiescent during Tito's reign, emerged rapidly. Renewed interest in national literature, poetry, and songs developed in each of the republics of Yugoslavia, though primarily in Croatia, Serbia, and Slovenia. In Croatia and Slovenia, nationalism was linked to the desire for an independent state; in Serbia, nationalism was coupled with calls for a stronger central Yugoslav state.[21]

---

[19] U.S. Agency for International Development, *Assistance for Victims of Atrocities in Croatia and Bosnia-Herzegovina,* unpublished paper, Washington, D.C., March 3, 1993, pp. 26-27. Also, see M.I. Roemer, *National Health Care Systems of the World: The Countries* (Oxford: Oxford University Press, 1991), pp. 256-258.

[20] *Assistance for Victims of Atrocities in Croatia and Bosnia-Herzegovina,* p. 27.

[21] S.P. Ramet, *Balkan Babel: Politics, Culture, and Religion in Yugoslavia* (Boulder: Westview Press, 1992).

Under these circumstances, nationalist leaders in each republic acquired power.[22] Spurred by their leaders, the people in the Yugoslav republics rekindled the ethnic animosities which had caused pain and bloodshed in the past. In 1990, the newly-elected Croatian Democratic Alliance in Croatia ratified new amendments which provided for the adoption of traditional Croatian ethnic symbols (a coat of arms, a flag, and an anthem) similar to those used by the Croatian Ustashe. The new government also refused to guarantee minority rights to Serbs living in Croatia (about twelve percent of the Croatian population).[23]

After consolidating power in 1987, Serbian President Slobodan Milošević enacted a series of "reforms" revoking autonomous status for both Kosovo and Vojvodina provinces. He appealed to Serbian pride by emphasizing the use of Cyrillic script, one of the two official alphabets. He also developed new ties to the Serbian Orthodox Church, reviving aspirations of a "Greater Serbia."

Meanwhile, Bosnia-Herzegovina began splintering along ethnic lines. In 1991, President Alija Izetbegović, fearful of Serbia's claim for a "Greater Serbia," declared that if the republics of Slovenia and Croatia seceded from Yugoslavia, the Republic of Bosnia-Herzegovina would also proclaim its independence. Two weeks later, Radovan Karadžić, a psychiatrist and leader of the Serbian Democratic Party in Bosnia, said that if Bosnia-Herzegovina seceded from Yugoslavia, the Bosnian Serbs would secede from Bosnia-Herzegovina. As the Bosnian Serbs did

---

[22] A. Borden, B. Cohen, M. Crevatin, D. Zmiarevic, eds., *Breakdown: War and Reconstruction in Yugoslavia* (London: War and Peace Reporting/War Report, 1992).

[23] L. Cohen, *Regime Transition in a Disintegrating Yugoslavia: The Law of Rule vs. the Rule of Law* (Pittsburgh: Center for Russian and East European Studies, 1992), p. 12.

not inhabit any contiguous geographic unit, the stage was set for war.

Outbreak of War

Fighting broke out in the former Yugoslavia three days after Slovenia and Croatia declared independence on June 25, 1991.[24] The Yugoslav Peoples' Army (JNA) attacked Slovenia, but soon abandoned war efforts there to concentrate on Croatia.

In the meantime, a referendum on independence was held in Bosnia-Herzegovina on February 29 and March 1, 1992. Bosnian Muslims and Croats overwhelmingly voted in favor of independence, but most Bosnian Serbs boycotted the referendum and declared it invalid. The Bosnian Serbs insisted that they wanted to remain part of a federal Yugoslavia and declared that they were forming their own state within the borders of Bosnia, called the Serbian Republic of Bosnia-Herzegovina, with Sarajevo as their capital.

Full scale war in Bosnia-Herzegovina[25] commenced in April 1992, almost simultaneous with international recognition of

---

[24] The European Community recognized Slovenia and Croatia as independent states on January 15, 1992.

[25] The former Yugoslav republic of Bosnia-Herzegovina is a union of two provinces: Herzegovina (a region located in the south-southwest of the republic), and Bosnia (which encompasses all territory not part of Herzegovina). Bosnia-Herzegovina's total population is 4.35 million. Prior to the war, 43.7 percent were Slavic Muslims, 31.3 percent Serbs, and 17.3 percent Croats. The various ethnic groups were intermingled throughout the country, although in some areas one ethnic group formed a significant majority.

the republic's independence.[26] JNA units stationed in Bosnia-Herzegovina joined Bosnian Serb irregular forces in attacks against the Bosnian government, Bosnian Croats, and Croatian Army units sent from neighboring Croatia. In the meantime, the republics of Serbia and Montenegro proclaimed the establishment of a new, truncated Yugoslavia, shorn of Macedonia, Croatia, Slovenia, and Bosnia-Herzegovina.[27]

International Intervention

The United Nations dispatched peacekeeping forces to Croatia and later to Bosnia-Herzegovina in early 1992.[28] The world body sought to achieve three goals in the former Yugoslavia: to create conditions of peace and security required for the negotiation of an overall settlement; to protect populations in UN Protected Areas (UNPA); and to assist UN humanitarian

---

[26] The European Community recognized Bosnia-Herzegovina's independence on April 6, 1992. The next day, the United States extended recognition to the new state, as did Croatia. Members of the international community, including the Arab world, soon followed suit. On May 22, 1992, Bosnia-Herzegovina was admitted as a member state to the United Nations. "Under international law, a state is an entity that has defined territory and a permanent population, under the control of its own government, and that engages in, or has the capacity to engage in, formal relations with other such entities." (See Section 201, *Restatement of the Foreign Relations Law of the United States,* Volume 1, Sections 1-488, as adopted and promulgated by the American Law Institute, Washington, D.C., May 14, 1986.)

[27] Human Rights Watch/Helsinki, *War Crimes in Bosnia-Herzegovina (Volume I),* pp. 19-31.

[28] The concept for the UNPROFOR plan is set forth in Annex III of the *Report of the Secretary-General Pursuant to Security Council Resolution 721 (1991),* United Nations Security Council, S/23280, December 11, 1991.

agencies in the return of all displaced persons who wish to return to their homes in these UNPAs.

In Croatia, the 14,000-member force, formally referred to as the United Nations Protection Force (UNPROFOR), was to monitor and help maintain a fragile cease-fire until a political solution could be reached between the Croatian government and the Serbs who had seized control of a third of the country. The UN forces created United Nations Protected Areas (UNPAs) in eastern Slavonia, western Slavonia, and the Serbian self-proclaimed "Krajina" region--all areas where Serbs constitute a majority or substantial minority. The UN forces were also charged with responsibility for demilitarizing the UNPAs by ensuring the withdrawal of JNA troops and demobilizing all armed groups.

UN peacekeeping troops began arriving in Sarajevo in March 1992. By establishing its headquarters in the Bosnian capital, the UNPROFOR mission hoped its presence would discourage further Serbian attacks. Such a hope was soon dashed, as Bosnian Serb forces assumed military and political control over parts of Bosnia-Herzegovina and laid siege to the capital of Sarajevo. Shelling of Sarajevo was so fierce that UN troops found they could not even protect their own vehicles and supplies.

The UN evacuated Sarajevo on May 16, 1992. Two hundred UN soldiers and staff members left the city and the UNPROFOR mission's headquarters was moved to Belgrade and Zagreb. One hundred and twenty UN troops remained in Sarajevo to assist relief convoys and to seek a lasting cease-fire in Bosnia-Herzegovina. Meanwhile, the United States began to pressure its allies to impose sanctions on Yugoslavia.

On May 30, 1992, three days after the Bosnian Serbs launched a mortar attack on a crowded marketplace in Sarajevo, killing at least twenty civilians, the UN Security Council voted to impose economic and other sanctions on the Federal Republic of

Yugoslavia (Serbia and Montenegro). The resolution required Yugoslavia "to cease all interference in Bosnia-Herzegovina and to use its influence to promote a general cease-fire, oversee the disbanding and disarming of elements of the JNA and irregular forces, and end efforts to create a purely Serbian enclave by driving out other ethnic groups."[29]

If the United Nations had hoped to avert a war in Bosnia-Herzegovina, it was now apparent that it had failed. Sarajevo was under siege, and UN forces maintained only nominal control of the city's airport for the delivery of humanitarian aid.

Some of Sarajevo's suffering was the result of actions of the Bosnian government. At the outbreak of the war, the government relied on the Sarajevo underworld to defend the city from Serb attacks. These militia forces took their toll on the city's population, especially Serbs, by looting and killing. Bosnian government forces, whether out of individual greed or official policy, shelled the Sarajevo airport, the city's primary lifeline for relief supplies. The shelling closed the airport for a time, driving up the price of black-market goods that entered the city via routes controlled by Bosnian army commanders and government officials. On June 16, 1992, Bosnian President Alija Izetbegović announced a military alliance with neighboring Croatia against Bosnian Serb and Yugoslav forces. Four days later, he formally declared the country to be in a state of war.

The Laws of War

Since the onset of war in the former Yugoslavia, the warring parties have been governed by the laws of war. This body of law is comprised, *inter alia*, of the four 1949 Geneva

---

[29] Paul Lewis, "UN Votes 13-0 for Embargo on Trade with Yugoslavia; Air Travel and Oil Curbed," *New York Times*, May 31, 1992.

Conventions, the two 1977 Protocols additional to those Conventions, and the customary laws of war.[30] A parallel field of law, known as "Hague Law," focuses less on targets and more on specific weapons; it seeks to limit the means and methods of conducting warfare, such as the deployment of poison gas and the placement of landmines, and the proportional harm they may inflict on civilians.[31]

Since 1977, the International Committee of the Red Cross (ICRC) has sought to merge the fields of law into a single body known as "international humanitarian law." Humanitarian law also seeks to incorporate key aspects of international human rights law, which sets out several absolute prohibitions on certain government actions, such as torture and arbitrary executions.

International humanitarian law distinguishes between international and non-international (internal) armed conflicts occurring in the territory of a single state, and the rules governing each type of conflict vary significantly. The United Nations[32] and international human rights organizations[33] have categorized the major wars in the former Yugoslavia as international armed conflicts. As a result, the warring parties (Yugoslavia, Slovenia,

---

[30] See W.M. Reisman and C.T. Antoniou, eds., *The Laws of War: A Comprehensive Collection of Primary Documents on International Laws Governing Armed Conflict* (New York: Vintage Books, 1994).

[31] For a discussion of "Hague Law," see The Arms Project of Human Rights Watch and Physicians for Human Rights, *Landmines: A Deadly Legacy*, (New York: Human Rights Watch, 1993), p. 313.

[32] See *Interim Report of the Commission of Experts Established Pursuant to Security Council Resolution 780 (1992)*, January 26, 1993, S/25274, p. 14, para. 45.

[33] See Human Rights Watch/Helsinki, *War Crimes in Bosnia-Herzegovina*, p. 202.

Croatia, and Bosnia-Herzegovina)[34] can be held accountable for any "grave breaches" of the four Geneva Conventions of 1949, the 1977 Protocols to those Conventions,[35] and to laws and customs of war.

Grave breaches are major violations of international humanitarian law which may be punished by any State on the basis of universal jurisdiction. Grave breaches prohibit wilful killing; torture; rape or inhuman treatment of protected persons, including biological experiments; unlawful deportation or transfer; unlawful confinement; wilfully causing great suffering or serious injury to body or health; depriving a protected person of the right to a fair and regular trial; the taking of hostages; and extensive destruction and appropriation of property, not justified by military necessity and carried out unlawfully and wantonly.

The Geneva Convention recognized that "military necessity" had its limits and that combatants who were wounded

---

[34] All parties to the conflict are High Contracting Parties to the Geneva Conventions and the Additional Protocols.

Geneva Conventions		Protocols I/II
Yugoslavia	(Ratification) April 21, 1950	June 11, 1979
Slovenia	(Succession) March 26, 1992	March 26, 1992
Croatia	(Succession) May 11, 1992	May 11, 1992
Bosnia-Herz.	(Succession) December 31, 1992	Dec 31, 1992

[35] Grave breaches are listed in Article 50 of the First Geneva Convention (wounded and sick), Article 51 of the Second Geneva Convention (maritime), Article 130 of the Third Geneva Convention (prisoners of war), and Article 147 of the Fourth Geneva Convention (civilians) of 1949. Grave breaches are also listed in Articles 11, paragraph 4, and 85 of Additional Protocol I of 1977. The grave breaches provisions are only relevant during an international armed conflict.

or held as prisoners of war (*hors de combat*) should not be military targets and should be treated humanely at all times. Broadening the concept of immune targets to a notion of immune objectives, the Convention declared that medical personnel, and equipment bearing the distinctive red cross symbol (later to be joined by the red crescent) which removed the wounded from the field, should be considered immune from attack.

The Geneva Conventions and the 1977 Protocols[35] provide that warring factions have an obligation to protect civilians, the sick and wounded, combatants who are *hors de combat*, and medical and religious personnel. All sides in a conflict must protect and limit damage to certain objects, including: medical facilities and ambulances; buildings designated as cultural or historical landmarks; facilities and transport used by humanitarian and relief agencies; and objects indispensable to the survival of the civilian population--such as crops, livestock, and drinking water installations.

Adherence to these conventions and protocols is largely dependent on the political will of civilian and military leaders who are parties to the conflict, the quality of military discipline these leaders maintain within their ranks, and the level of political and economic pressure outside governments and the United Nations can assert on the warring parties.

---

[35] See W. M. Reisman and C.T. Antoniou, eds., *The Laws of War*.

III. WAR CRIMES, CRIMES AGAINST HUMANITY, AND GENOCIDE

United Nations personnel were aware of massive violations of human rights and humanitarian law in the former Yugoslavia soon after fighting broke out between the Yugoslav Peoples' Army (JNA) and Croatian forces in 1991. In August 1991, JNA and Serb irregular forces began their siege of Vukovar, a city of 50,000 on Croatia's eastern border. For three months the JNA and paramilitary forces shelled the city, killing hundreds of civilians and causing extensive physical damage. When Vukovar fell to the Serbs on November 19, 1991, the UN Secretary-General's personal envoy to the former Yugoslavia, Cyrus Vance, intervened to help facilitate the evacuation of hundreds of patients from the city hospital. He later learned that just hours before the evacuation, JNA and Serb irregular forces had removed over 200 patients and staff from the hospital and executed them outside the city.

UN soldiers and civilian personnel, deployed in the United Nations Protected Areas (UNPAs) in March and April 1992, witnessed or heard accounts of massive expulsions of Serbs and non-Serbs from their homes and villages. Several UN field staff later told human rights investigators[36] that they had reported these abuses to their superiors, but were told they were not empowered at the time to do anything to stop or prevent the expulsions. More intent on brokering peace in the former Yugoslavia than publicly criticizing the warring factions, UN officials presented complaints of violations of human rights in

---

[36] Physicians for Human Rights representatives heard such complaints from UN staff in UNPA sectors east and west. Helsinki Watch representatives also reported similar complaints. See Helsinki Watch, *War Crimes in Bosnia-Herzegovina*, p. 171.

separate reports to the Croatian and Serbian governments but never made the information public, nor publicly condemned such abuses.

The world first learned of atrocities in the former Yugoslavia not through the United Nations but through the courageous efforts of print and television journalists. *New York Newsday* reporter, Roy Gutman, won a Pulitzer Prize for his coverage, in July 1992, of the appalling conditions and treatment of Croat and Muslim detainees held in Serb-run detention camps near the towns of Banja Luka and Trnopolje in northwestern Bosnia.[37] After Gutman and freelance photographer Andrée Kaiser visited the Manjaca and Omarska camps, international pressure led to visits by the International Committee of the Red Cross (ICRC) and the foreign press corps.

For weeks afterwards, television viewers around the world saw horrifying images of prison camps. The British network ITN convinced the Banja Luka authorities to provide access to Omarska camp. The guards allowed them to photograph some prisoners being rushed through meals. One of the most wrenching scenes showed hundreds of emaciated men behind barbed wire, their eyes hollowed from hunger and despair. Most of the detainees were terrified and refused to speak to foreigners, although some, once out of the presence of the guards, whispered accounts of the atrocities they had suffered or witnessed.

Only after reports of conditions in the camps appeared in the press did the United Nations take seriously its obligation to investigate war crimes and crimes against humanity in the former

---

[37] Roy Gutman's first articles on conditions in the Serb camps, entitled "Hidden Horror" and "Witness Tells of Serbian Death Camp," appeared in the July 19, 1992 edition of *New York Newsday*.

Yugoslavia.[38] On October 6, 1992, the Security Council established a Commission of Experts to investigate and collect evidence of "grave breaches of the Geneva Conventions and other violations of humanitarian law" in the Yugoslav conflicts. It was an extraordinary act. Not since the International Military Tribunal at Nuremberg[39] had the world community taken collective action to provide for an international body to investigate violations of international humanitarian law, with a view to prosecuting its perpetrators before an ad hoc international tribunal.

Based in Geneva, the Commission began collecting reports of human rights violations in the former Yugoslavia from news agencies and human rights organizations. Physicians for Human Rights (PHR) entered into a contractual agreement with the Commission to send forensic teams to the former republic to investigate mass graves believed to be associated with war crimes.

Following the submission of the Commission's *First Interim Report*, the UN Security Council voted, on February 11, 1992, to establish an ad hoc criminal tribunal to prosecute war crimes, crimes against humanity, and acts of genocide in the

---

[38] In July 1992, the United Nations Commission on Human Rights appointed Tadeusz Mazowiecki, a former prime minister of Poland, as a special rapporteur to investigate human rights abuses in the former Yugoslavia. Despite inadequate funding and logistical support, Mazowiecki managed to bring public attention to atrocities committed in the former federation. In July 1995, Mazowiecki resigned in protest of the West's failure to use military force to protect so-called UN "safe areas" in eastern Bosnia.

[39] Agreement for the Prosecution and Punishment of the Major War Criminals of the European Axis, August 8, 1945, 82 U.N.T.S. 279 (London Agreement). For the Charter of the International Military Tribunal at Nuremberg see W.M. Reisman and C.T. Antoniou, *The Laws of War*, pp. 316-322.

former Yugoslavia.[40] The UN Security Council declared that a primary objective of the International Criminal Tribunal for the former Yugoslavia would be to establish individual responsibility for crimes in order to avoid the attribution of collective guilt to any specific ethnic group.

The International Criminal Tribunal's statute adopted the definitions of war crimes and crimes against humanity contained in the London Charter of the International Military Tribunal, drafted by the World War II Allied powers in 1945 to establish the Nuremberg Tribunal. The Charter categorized "war crimes" as violations that shall include, but not be limited to:

> murder; ill-treatment or deportation to slave labour, or for any other purpose of the civilian population of or in an occupied territory; murder or ill-treatment of prisoners of war or persons on the seas; killing of hostages; plunder of public or private property; wanton destruction of cities, towns or villages; or devastation not justified by military necessity.[41]

Article 6 of the London Charter defined "crimes against humanity" as:

> murder, extermination, enslavement, deportation, and other inhumane acts committed against any civilian population, before or during the war; or persecutions on political, racial, or religious grounds in execution of, or in connection with,

---

[40] United Nations, *Security Council Resolution 808* (1992).

[41] See W.M. Reisman and C.T. Antoniou, eds., *The Laws of War*, pp. 318-322.

any crime...whether or not in violation of the domestic law of the country where perpetrated.[42]

The term "civilian" is defined in the London Charter as anyone who never took part in hostilities and combatants who are *hors de combat*.

"Genocide," the most heinous of all the crimes in the International Criminal Tribunal's statute, is defined in Article II of the "Convention on the Prevention and Punishment of the Crime of Genocide," adopted by the UN General Assembly on December 9, 1948 (See Appendix F):

> [A]ny of the following acts committed with intent to destroy, in whole or in part, a national, ethnic, racial or religious group as such: (a) Killing members of the group; (b) Causing serious bodily or mental harm to members of the group; (c) Deliberately inflicting on the group conditions of life calculated to bring about its physical destruction in whole or in part; (d) Imposing measures intending to prevent births within the group; (e) Forcibly transferring children of the group to another group.

The Commission of Experts completed its work in April 1994 and submitted 65,000 pages of documents and 300 hours of videotape to the International Criminal Tribunal. In the Commission's records was evidence of some 150 mass graves and detailed dossiers on 900 prison camps and 90 paramilitary groups throughout the former Yugoslavia. The Commission concluded that Bosnian Serb forces were guilty of "crimes against humanity," and charged that Bosnian Serb army and irregular forces may have committed genocide in the Prijedor region. The Commission also

---

[42] Ibid.

said that the Bosnian Serb high command may have directed "a systematic rape policy."[43]

Prosecuting War Criminals

The International Criminal Tribunal, led by a highly respected South African judge, Richard Goldstone, needs the cooperation of the authorities in Serbia, Bosnia-Herzegovina, and Croatia (some of whom could turn out to be potential suspects themselves), in handing over defendants to stand trial in The Hague where the courtroom is located. At the time of this writing (May 1996) fifty-seven people have been indicted by the court, most of them Bosnian Serbs but also a few Bosnian Croats, Bosnian Muslims, and three senior JNA officials from Serbia. Only one of them, Dusan Tadic, a Bosnian Serb guard who worked in the notorious Omarska camp and was later arrested in Germany, has been charged in court.[44] Two Bosnian Croats and two Bosnian Muslims are also in custody at the Tribunal's detention center. The other suspects are still at large, presumably in the territory of the former Yugoslavia.

The International Criminal Tribunal will hold no trials *in absentia*, but prosecutors can hold a public proceeding with witnesses to confirm evidence and issue international arrest warrants. As there are no statutes of limitation governing war crimes and the other crimes contained in the International Criminal Tribunal's statute, the arrest warrants will remain in effect as long as necessary.

---

[43] *Final Report of the Commission of Experts Established Pursuant to Security Council Resolution 780 (1992)*, S/1994/674, 27 May 1994 and Annexes, S/1994/674/Add.2(Vol. I-V), December 28, 1994.

[44] R. Cohen, "Bosnian Serb Denies All At A War Crimes Tribunal," *New York Times*, April 27, 1995.

Among the defendants are Radovan Karadžić, President of the self-declared Bosnian Serb state, and General Ratko Mladić, the commander of the Bosnian Serb army. Both men were charged on July 25, 1995 with genocide, crimes against humanity, and war crimes.[45] In its indictment,[46] the International Criminal Tribunal said that Karadžić and Mladić,

> individually, or in concert with others, planned, instigated, ordered, or otherwise aided and abetted, in the planning, preparation, and execution of the persecutions, on political and religious grounds, of Bosnian Muslim and Bosnian Croat civilians, or knew, or had reason to know, that subordinates were about to do the same, or had done so, and failed to take the necessary and reasonable measures to prevent such acts or to punish the perpetrators thereof.

The International Criminal Tribunal charged that acts of genocide and crimes against humanity committed by Karadžić and Mladić involved:

> (1) the internment of thousands of Bosnian Muslims and Croats in detention facilities where they were subjected to widespread acts of physical and psychological abuse and to inhumane conditions;

> (2) the targeting of Bosnian Muslim and Bosnian Croat communities, and in particular their political leaders, intellectuals and professionals;

---

[45] M. Simons, "U.N. Tribunal Indicts Bosnian Serb Leader and a Commander," *New York Times*, July 26, 1995.

[46] Indictments, United Nations International Criminal Tribunal for the former Yugoslavia, IT/95/5/D337-D315, July 24, 1995.

(3) the deportation of thousands of Bosnian
Muslim and Bosnian Croat civilians, including
women, children, and elderly persons who were taken
directly from their homes;

(4) the shelling of civilian gatherings in Sarajevo,
Srebrenica, and Tuzla, in order to kill, terrorize,
and demoralize the civilian population;

(5) the appropriation and plunder of real and
personal property of Bosnian Muslim and Bosnian
Croat civilians;

(6) the persecution of civilians, including the
systematic destruction of Bosnian Muslim and
Bosnian Croat homes and businesses in order to
ensure that the inhabitants could not and would not
return to their homes and communities; and,

(7) the systematic damaging or destruction of
sacred sites, both Muslim and Roman Catholic.

The International Criminal Tribunal's indictment of Dr.
Karadžić and General Mladić on charges of genocide is historic.
Never before had an international tribunal indicted top civilian and
military leaders for acts of genocide.

On November 15, 1995, the International Criminal
Tribunal issued additional charges of genocide against Karadžić
and Mladić for the alleged execution of 6,000 to 8,700 Bosnian
government soldiers and civilians who have been missing since
Bosnian Serb forces seized the UN safe haven of Srebrenica in
July 1995.[47] The indictment charged that the attack was

---

[47] Indictments, United Nations International Criminal Tribunal
for the former Yugoslavia, IT/95/18/I/D338-D325, November 15, 1995.

authorized by Dr. Karadžić and carried out by forces under the command of General Mladić, who was seen at several sites of systematic mass killings.

In August 1995, the U.S. government released to the UN Security Council several spy satellite photographs showing large mounds of freshly-dug earth on farm land near Srebrenica. The mounds had not been there when spy planes and satellites surveyed the sites just after Srebrenica was overrun by Bosnian Serb forces, but showed up in photographs taken several days later.[48]

American officials believe there may be as many as ten mass burial sites in the area of Srebrenica.[49] They also suspect that Bosnian Serb soldiers have tried to destroy evidence of the executions by pouring corrosive chemicals over the bodies and scattering corpses that previously had been buried in mass graves.

The Dayton Accords

On November 21, 1995, after twenty-one days of talks, the presidents of Bosnia-Herzegovina, Croatia, and Serbia initialed a peace agreement in Dayton, Ohio, ending nearly four years of war in the former Yugoslavia.[50] The American-brokered agreement took effect when it was formally signed in Paris on December 14, 1995 by Alija Izetbegović, president of Bosnia-Herzegovina, Franjo Tudjman. president of Croatia, and Slobodan

---

[48] B. Crossette, "U.S. Seeks to Prove Mass Killings," *New York Times*, August 11, 1995.

[49] T. Weiner, "U.S. Says Serbs May have Tried to Destroy Massacre Evidence," *New York Times*, October 30, 1995.

[50] E. Sciolino, "Accord Reached to End the War in Bosnia; Clinton Pledges U.S. Troops to Keep Peace," *New York Times*, November 22, 1995.

Milošević, president of Serbia. The peace accord allowed for the deployment in Bosnia of 60,000 NATO troops.

The Dayton settlement was a compromise among conflicting aims. For the Bosnian government, it affirmed the legal integrity of the country and restored the unity of the capital, Sarajevo. The Bosnian Serbs received--if not the separate state they wanted--a semi-autonomous republic, Republika Srpska, comprising forty-nine percent of the territory of Bosnia-Herzegovina. The other fifty-one percent is comprised of the Federation of Bosnia and Herzegovina, which is a U.S.-brokered Muslim-Croat federation.

Under the peace accords, people indicted by the International Criminal Tribunal cannot hold elected office. The governments have pledged to cooperate with the International Criminal Tribunal, but are not explicitly required to arrest indicted people. Meanwhile, the NATO force, including about 20,000 American troops, will have the responsibility to detain and turn over indicted war criminals to the International Criminal Tribunal, but only if it comes into contact with them or its deployment is obstructed by them.[51]

"Ethnic Cleansing"

"Ethnic cleansing" is one of the most appalling aspects of the wars in the former Yugoslavia. Originally a Chetnik term (*ciscenje terena*-"cleansing of the ground"[52]), Serb leaders have used it since the onset of the war in June 1991 to describe their

---

[51] R. Cohen, "France to Rejoin Military Command of NATO Alliance," *New York Times*, December 6, 1995, p. A1.

[52] L. Silber, A. Little, *Yugoslavia: Death of a Nation* (New York: TV Books, 1995), p. 171.

campaign to establish homogenous control over geographic areas by terrorizing and forcibly displacing non-Serbs. (By mid-1992, as the phrase began to take on a special horror of its own, some Serb leaders came to prefer the euphemism "ethnic shifting.") Victims of "ethnic cleansing" have been expelled from their homes, held in detention camps, deported, killed in indiscriminate attacks, raped and tortured, and summarily executed.

All parties to the conflict in the former Yugoslavia are guilty of forcibly displacing large numbers of people based on their religion and ethnicity. However, until the large displacement of Serbs from the area referred to as the Krajina region of Croatia in August 1995, the chief offenders throughout the conflict were Bosnian Serb military and paramilitary forces.

The pattern of "ethnic cleansing" by Bosnian Serb forces in several different regions of Bosnia-Herzegovina has followed a similar pattern.[53] The process often begins with an attempt to terrorize civilians through direct shelling and sniper attacks.[54] The attacks initially involve light and heavy artillery, which often is used indiscriminately to force the population from the besieged area. Sometimes attacks are conducted on religious holidays when people are gathered in groups. This was the case in June 1993, when a Serbian shell killed at least twelve civilians and wounded eighty others who had gathered on a Muslim holy day to watch a soccer match in Sarajevo.[55]

---

[53] For a detailed account of the process of "ethnic cleansing" in Bosnia-Herzegovina, see Helsinki Watch, *War Crimes in Bosnia-Herzegovina* (Volume II), pp. 10-16.

[54] According to Article 147 of the Fourth Geneva Convention, "extensive destruction and appropriation of property, not justified by military necessity and carried out unlawfully and wantonly" is considered a "grave breach" of the Geneva Conventions of 1949.

[55] C. Sudetic, "Mortar Fire Kills 12 at Soccer Game in Bosnian Capital," *New York Times,* June 2, 1993.

After Bosnian Serb forces occupy an area, the remaining residents are taken from their homes, separated by sex and age, and taken to places of detention. In some cases, residents are interrogated immediately after their arrest and shot. Women and young girls are often raped. In the detention centers and concentration camps, detainees are usually registered, interrogated, physically and psychologically abused, and, in some cases, summarily executed. Those who survive internment are usually placed on buses, trains, or cattle cars and taken to the front lines, where they are exchanged, or forced to walk, sometimes through minefields, to Muslim- or Croatian-controlled territory.

While "ethnic cleansing" has been overwhelmingly a Bosnian Serb practice, Croatian, Bosnian Croat, and Bosnian government forces have also forced people to flee from areas under their control. In June 1992, Serbs were evicted from Mostar by Bosnian Croat forces. In June 1993, Bosnian Croat forces began evicting Muslim residents from the west side of Mostar. After thousands of Muslims fled across the historic Stari Most bridge to the eastern bank, their attackers destroyed the bridge.[56] From then on, the Bosnian Croats interfered with the delivery of food and medical aid to the civilian population on the eastern side of the city. On December 23, 1993, the Bosnian Croats refused to allow delivery of materials for a field hospital to the displaced population. Moreover, vehicles clearly marked with red cross emblems were fired upon in repeated attacks.[57]

---

[56] *Final Report of the Commission of Experts Established Pursuant to Security Council Resolution 780 (1992), op. cit.,* "Destruction of Cultural Property," p. 68, para. 295-297.

[57] United Nations Commission on Human Rights, *Sixth Periodic Report*, "Situation of Human Rights in the Territory of the former Yugoslavia submitted by Mr. Tadeusz Mazowiecki, Special Rapporteur," February 21, 1994, p. 13, and *Eighth Periodic Report*, August 1994, p. 4.

Croatian government forces have been guilty of forcibly displacing tens of thousands of ethnic Serbs since the war began in 1991. The most serious incident of "ethnic cleansing" took place between May and August 1995, when 200,000 ethnic Serbs fled from the region referred to as the Krajina region of Croatia in advance of a massive Croatian military offensive. During the operation Croatian troops looted and burned Serb homes and villages. Soldiers also fired into lines of fleeing Serb civilians crossing the border between Croatia and Bosnia-Herzegovina. In the border town of Dovr, UN troops reported seeing five elderly and handicapped Serbs pulled from a school and killed.[58]

Bosnian government forces have forcibly displaced civilian populations, although not in a fashion or on a scale that remotely parallels the Bosnian Serb policy of "ethnic cleansing." In June 1993, after Bosnian Croat forces had "cleansed" Mostar, Vitez, and Prozor, Bosnian government troops began expelling Croat civilians from Travnik.[59] At approximately the same time, 15,000 Croatian refugees fled the Karanj area, which was under Bosnian government fire. British UN forces said they saw Bosnian government troops shooting machine guns at Croatian civilians fleeing Guca Gora.[60] The UN also faults the Bosnian government for deaths occurring in the winter of 1994 when it deprived residents of Banocuci, Drin, Nova Bita, and Pazaric access to medical and food supplies.[61]

---

[58] R. Bonner, "Frightened and Jeered At, Serbs Flee From Croatia," *New York Times*, August 10, 1995.

[59] C. Sudetic, "Serbs and Croats Mount Joint Attack on Muslim Town," *New York Times*, June 28, 1993.

[60] C. Sudetic, "Croatian Forces Face Muslim Army," *New York Times*, June 9, 1993.

[61] Commission on Human Rights, *Sixth Periodic Report*, p. 13.

The Scope of Forced Displacement

"Ethnic cleansing" has caused widespread displacement throughout the former Yugoslavia, but especially in Bosnia-Herzegovina. The summer of 1994 saw brutal consequences for Bosnian non-Serbs. Ninety-eight hundred non-Serbs, mostly Muslim, were displaced from areas of Bosnia under Serb control.[62] By September 1994, 657,000 non-Serbs (eighty-nine percent) of a pre-war population of 737,000 in northern and eastern Bosnia, had fled or had been forced to flee their homes and villages.

As of December 1995, fighting and "ethnic cleansing" in all of Bosnia had displaced or affected 2,749,000 people, or sixty-three percent of the country's pre-war population of 4,350,000.[63]

Physical Abuse and Summary Executions

"Ethnic cleansing" is usually accompanied by physical abuse, including torture, and summary executions, as the advancing forces enter civilian areas. Many of these acts of violence are carried out with extreme brutality in order to instill terror in the civilian population and cause them to flee.

PHR representatives were able to reconstruct a composite account of "ethnic cleansing" in northwestern Bosnia, based on extensive interviews with refugees from Prijedor, a district in the area known as the Krajina region of Bosnia. The interviewees

---

[62] See "Grim Numbers," Refugees International, September 22, 1994. Statistics on forcible displacement have been compiled regularly by Bosnia Relief Watch, a project of Refugees International, Washington, D.C.

[63] United Nations High Commissioner for Refugees, "Beneficiaries within former Yugoslavia," *Information Notes*, December 1995, p. 5.

were from the towns of Sanski Most, Prijedor, Klujc, and Ljubija.[64] In some cases, interviewees were examined medically to confirm signs of trauma. While dates or specific incidents differed from town to town, the pattern of abuses was remarkably consistent.

Local Bosnian Serb officials began their "ethnic cleansing" campaign in the Prijedor district in early 1992.[65] A Bosnian Serb paramilitary group took control of the district's television transmitter and blocked programs from Sarajevo and Zagreb. Residents could only receive programs from Belgrade and later Banja Luka. The television programs from Belgrade insinuated that non-Serbs wanted war and threatened the Serbs. Next, local Serbs took control of Radio Prijedor. Radio announcers slandered former non-Serbian leaders by criticizing everything from their alleged lack of efficiency to their private lives. They also claimed that dangerous Muslim extremists were in the area, preparing genocide against the Serbs.

By May 1992, most non-Serbs with white collar jobs, including physicians, had been removed from their positions. Special documents were issued to non-Serbs, who were permitted to travel along the roads between Banja Luka, Sanski Most, and Prijedor. Checkpoints were set up along the roads to inspect the required documents. A former medical student at Banja Luka University described an incident in which fifteen Muslims were removed from a bus in the town of Rasavci because they did not have proper documents. They were taken to a football field and shot while the rest of the passengers watched.

When Bosnian Serb forces captured the town of Prijedor, they took special care to detain "all the prominent people of

---

[64] The interviews were conducted in January 1993.

[65] *Final Report of the Commission of Experts Established Pursuant to Security Council Resolution 780 (1992)*, pp. 37-43.

Prijedor," as one former resident of the town told PHR. This included health professionals, such as internist Osman Mahmuljan, gynecologist Zeljko Sikora, and ear-nose-and-throat specialist Esad Sadikovic.

According to journalist Roy Gutman, "the underlying pattern...was to round up the most educated, the most wealthy, the most successful, and the political and religious leadership from previously prepared lists."[66] The mayor was deported to the notorious Omarska detention camp, while his wife, a physician and medical director of the Prijedor hospital, was told not to report to work. On May 28, 1992, all hospital personnel were stopped on their way to work and divided into groups based on presumed ethnicity. Only Serbs were allowed into the hospital, while non-Serbs were either returned home or deported to detention camps.

Civilians who had not already fled the Prijedor region were often beaten or killed. A woman from Ljubija told PHR that a soldier wearing a JNA uniform hit her front teeth with the butt of a gun and broke her finger while removing her wedding ring; the gaping hole where her front teeth had been and the flexion deformity of her ring finger were consistent with her account.

A 24-year-old woman described to PHR events in Ljubija in August 1992 which she believed amounted to a mass execution:

> At five o'clock in the afternoon I was sitting with some other people in the front of my house when I heard buses approaching. I saw two buses and a truck pass by filled with men who were holding their hands behind their heads. In each bus, there was a driver and three soldiers. They took the buses to the stadium. And I heard people singing

---

[66] R. Gutman, "Death Camp Lists: In Town After Town, Bosnia's Elite Disappeared," *New York Newsday*, November 8, 1992.

and somebody screaming "Sing! Sing!" They started singing, and then I heard screaming again-- "yii,yo,yii,yii." They were singing a Serbian song. The lyrics are: "Who is saying Serbia is a small country when it has been in the war three times." Then I heard shooting for about two minutes: Di di di di di di di di di di di di di di. I heard nothing after the shooting. In about fifteen minutes, I saw the buses drive away. There were no people on the buses, only the drivers.

Other former residents of Ljubija testified in separate interviews that a large number of bodies were buried in mines near the town. In January 1996, the Croatian Helsinki Committee for Human Rights estimated that as many as 8,000 bodies were in a mine and that it was likely to be the largest mass grave in Serb-held Bosnia and the central collection point for thousands of corpses that remain from the Bosnian Serbs' campaign of "ethnic cleansing" in northwestern Bosnia. At the time of this writing, PHR and the International Criminal Tribunal investigators were awaiting access to the area.[67]

In October and November 1995, a PHR forensic team, at the request of the International Criminal Tribunal for the former Yugoslavia, investigated several mass graves in northwestern Bosnia. The graves, which were located in territory held by the Bosnian Serbs until September 1995, are believed to contain the remains of civilians who were summarily executed between May and August 1992.

---

[67] C. Hedges, "Bosnian Mine Thought to Hold Mass Graves," *New York Times*, January 8, 1996.

Rape

Rape in war is an attempt to dominate, humiliate, and control the behavior of a woman and her family and community.[68] The intent of rape is not only to defile and destroy the individual woman but to destroy a woman's sense of self and identity. It can also be used to disable an enemy by destroying the bonds of family of entire communities. In situations of ethnic conflict, rape can be both a military strategy and a nationalistic policy. Rape of "enemy" women can be explicitly ordered or tacitly condoned by military authorities to promote hatred of another ethnic group.

All sides in the wars in the former Yugoslavia have used rape[69] as a weapon of war. Soldiers have raped women and young girls, often in front of their families and neighbors, as if they were "war booty." Women have been captured and raped during interrogation in makeshift detention centers. Women have

---

[68] A.E. Goldfeld, R.F. Mollica, B.H. Pesavento, and S.V. Farone, "The Physical and Psychological Sequelae of Torture," *The Journal of the American Medical Association* 259 (1988):2725-2729. Rape is also committed against men and children.

[69] Rape and sexual abuse constitute serious violations of international human rights and humanitarian law. Article 27(2) of the Fourth Geneva Convention states: "Women shall be especially protected against any attack on their honor." On this basis, the same provision prohibits, "in particular rape, enforced prostitution, or any form of indecent assault." Under an agreement reached under the auspices of the International Committee of the Red Cross in Geneva on May 22, 1992, all parties to the conflict in the former Yugoslavia promised to comply with the Fourth Geneva Convention. Article 147 of that Convention specifies that "torture or inhuman treatment" and "willfully causing great suffering or serious injury to body or health" are "grave breaches," and hence judicially actionable as war crimes.

been held in prison camps where they are placed in special rooms and gang-raped, often for several days at a time, by prison guards.

As a tool of "ethnic cleansing," rape has been used in the former Yugoslavia to intimidate and degrade women, and to humiliate their communities. The effect of rape is often to ensure that women and their families will flee and never return. A UN team that investigated allegations of rape in the former Yugoslavia found the following pattern during the siege of Vukovar in the summer of 1992:

> Serb paramilitary units would enter a village.
> Several women would be raped in the presence of
> others so that word spread throughout the village
> and a climate of fear was created. Several days
> later, Yugoslav Peoples' Army...officers would
> arrive at the village offering permission to the
> non-Serb population to leave the village. Those
> male villagers who wanted to stay then decided to leave
> with the women and children in order to protect them
> from being raped.[70]

The rape of women on a large scale suggests that local commanders must have known that their soldiers were raping women and took no steps to stop or prevent these abuses. Some reports indicate that commanders have at times even ordered soldiers to commit rapes.[71]

---

[70] *Report on the Situation of Human Rights in the Territory of the former Yugoslavia*, submitted by Mr. Tadeusz Mazowiecki, Special Rapporteur of the Commission on Human Rights, pursuant to Commission resolution 1992/S-1/1 of 14 August 1992, Annex II, para. 48(a), UN Doc. E/CN.4/1993/50.

[71] R. Gutman, "Rape Camps: Evidence in Bosnia Mass Attacks Points to Karadzic's Pals," *New York Newsday*, April 19, 1993, p. 7.

The number of rapes reported in the former Yugoslavia raises the question of whether such activity reflects policy. The UN Commission of Experts concluded that the Bosnian Serb high command may have directed "a systematic rape policy." If this can be proven, and if the element of intent to destroy or attempt to destroy a designated group in whole or in part is involved, then those responsible could be punished for genocide.

There have been difficulties in determining the extent of rape in the former Yugoslavia. A European Community report, charged with investigating the rape of Muslim women in Bosnia-Herzegovina and released in January 1993, estimated that 20,000 Muslim women had been raped by Serbian forces. The Bosnian government places the figure between 50,000 and 60,000 women and claims to have documentation on 13,000 cases of Muslim women violated by Serbs.[72] As this significantly smaller number of 13,000 suggests, the larger figures on rape are almost always based on extrapolations derived from a smaller number of known or reported occurrences.

The UN Commission on Human Rights has described the difficulties in obtaining accurate information on the extent of rape in the former Yugoslavia:[73]

> A persistent problem, undermining attempts to
> chart the extent of the incidence of rape and other
> forms of sexual abuse, remains the exceptional
> difficulty in obtaining reports of or investigating

---

[72] J. Laber, "Bosnia: Questions about Rape," *The New York Review of Books*, March 25, 1993, pp. 3-6.

[73] Rape of women including minors has occurred on a large scale. While the UN team of experts has found victims among all ethnic groups involved in the conflict, the majority of the rapes they have documented have been committed by Serb forces against Muslim women from Bosnia-Herzegovina. See: United Nations Economic and Social Council, E/CN.4/1993/50, February 10, 1993, p. 73.

allegations. Hindrances include the continued war conditions, the distress of victims and their fear of retaliation by or on behalf of the perpetrators, the dispersal of victims among other displaced people and, not least, the refusal of the Bosnian Serb authorities to permit investigations in territories under their control. Also, reports of incidents of rape often only come to the attention of investigators many months after the incident has occurred.[74]

While the true numbers of rape in the former Yugoslavia may be very high, unsubstantiated claims risk creating questions about the credibility of the numbers themselves. In January 1993, the UN sent a team of physicians and public health specialists, including PHR physician Shana Swiss,[75] to the former Yugoslavia to determine the scale of rape since the onset of the war in June 1991. The medical team collected data on abortions, deliveries, known pregnancies due to rape, and sexually-transmitted diseases. From a small sample of six hospitals in Bosnia-Herzegovina, Croatia, and Serbia, they identified 119 pregnancies that resulted from rape.

According to estimates established in previous medical studies,[76] a single act of unprotected intercourse will result in pregnancy between one percent and four percent of the time. Based on the assumption that one percent of acts of unprotected

---

[74] UN Commission on Human Rights, *Sixth Periodic Report*, op.cit., p. 11.

[75] At the time of the study, Dr. Swiss was the Director of the PHR Women's Program.

[76] See W. Cates, Jr. and C.A. Blackmore, "Sexual Assault and Sexually Transmitted Diseases," in K.K. Holmes, P.A. Mardh, P.F. Sparling and P.J. Wiesner, eds., *Sexually Transmitted Diseases* (New York: McGraw-Hill International Book Co., 1984), pp. 119-125.

intercourse result in pregnancy, the 119 identified pregnancies alone could be representative of some 11,900 rapes. Such a figure, the team concluded, indicated that the incidence of rape in the wars in the former Yugoslavia was systematic and widespread.

Dr. Swiss and psychologist Joan E. Giller later cautioned, in an article in the *Journal of the American Medical Association*, that any figures on the scale of rape in armed conflicts in the former Yugoslavia or elsewhere should be examined carefully:

> Under reporting, along with the reluctance of many physicians to ask women seeking abortions or perinatal care whether they had been raped during the war, would lead to an underestimate of the number of women raped. On the other hand, multiple and repeated rapes of the same women were frequently reported and could lead to an over-estimate of the number of women (as opposed to the number of incidents of rape) involved. The goal is not to come up with an exact number, which is impossible, but rather to use medical data to suggest a scale of violations that cannot be determined from individual testimonies.[77]

Based on interviews with 223 female and male victims and witnesses of rape and other forms of sexual assault residing in Croatia, Slovenia, and Bosnia-Herzegovina, the UN Commission of Experts found five patterns of rape in the former Yugoslavia. The first pattern involved individuals or small groups committing sexual assault in conjunction with looting and intimidation of the target ethnic group. The second pattern involved sexual assaults committed in conjunction with fighting in an area, often including the rape of women in public. The third pattern involved sexual

---

[77] S. Swiss and J.E. Giller, "Rape as a Crime of War: A Medical Perspective," *The Journal of the American Medical Association* 270 (1993):612-615. See Appendix A.

assaults in detention centers. The fourth pattern involved sexual assaults against women for the purpose of terrorizing and humiliating them, often as part of an "ethnic cleansing" campaign. The fifth pattern involved detention of women in hotels and similar facilities for sexual entertainment of soldiers. These women were more often killed than exchanged, unlike women in other camps.[78]

Rape carries with it traumatic social repercussions, which may be affected by a woman's cultural origins or social status. Relief and human rights organizations report that women who have survived rape are frequently reluctant to report the incidents, even after reaching places where they are safe, because they fear social stigmatization.[79] Some Bosnian rape victims have been harshly judged and even ostracized by members of their communities and families.

The UN Commission of Experts concluded that in Bosnia-Herzegovina:

> some of the reported rape and sexual assault cases committed by Serbs, mostly against Muslims, are clearly the result of individual or small group conduct without evidence of command direction or an overall policy. However, many more seem to be part of an overall pattern whose characteristics include...maximizing shame and humiliation to not only the victim, but also the victim's community...One factor in particular that leads to this conclusion is the large number of rapes which occurred in places of detention. These rapes do not appear to be random, and they indicate at least

---

[78] *Final Report of the Commission of Experts*, pp. 58-59.

[79] Amnesty International, *Bosnia-Herzegovina: Rape and Sexual Abuse by Armed Forces* (London: Amnesty International, 1993), p. 1.

a policy of encouraging rape supported by the deliberate failure of camp commanders and local authorities to exercise command and control over the personnel under their authority.[80]

Destruction of Cultural Property

Another feature of "ethnic cleansing" in the former Yugoslavia has been the deliberate destruction or damaging of cultural property. Bosnian Serb and Bosnian Croat forces have been especially guilty of targeting historical, religious, and ethnic landmarks not justified by military necessity.

During the 1991 siege of Dubrovnik in Croatia, JNA and Serbian paramilitary forces shelled the historic Old Town, hitting three out every five buildings. Included in the destruction was the ancient Franciscan Cathedral and Convent, St. Blaise's Church, and the historic foundation of Onofrio.[81] In another incident, on May 7, 1993, in Banja Luka, Bosnian Serbs destroyed the Arnajdija Mosque, built in 1587, and the Ferhad-Pasha Mosque, built in 1583.[82]

The Institute for the Protection of the Historic and Natural Cultural Heritage of Bosnia-Herzegovina has accused the Croatian Defence Council and the Croatian Army of destroying the Mostar bridge on November 9, 1993. Built between 1557 and 1566, the

---

[80] Annex, *Final Report of the Commission of Experts Established Pursuant to Security Council Resolution 780 (1992)*, UN Doc. S/1994/674, 27 May 1994, p. 60.

[81] Annex to the *Final Report of the Commission of Experts Established Pursuant to Security Council Resolution 780 (1992)*, "Destruction of Cultural Property," Section 3, para. 288-292.

[82] S. Kinzer, "2 Major Mosques Blown Up By Serbs," *New York Times*, May 8, 1993.

bridge was a symbol of Bosnia-Herzegovina which closed the gap between the Muslim and Croat communities. It embodied the links which united both peoples in spite of their religious differences.

Two PHR representatives witnessed massive destruction of property, including cultural monuments, during a tour of Vukovar in March 1993. The city had been subject to a three-month siege by JNA and Serbian paramilitary forces from August to November 1991. Inside the city's Roman Catholic cathedral, which was pitted with shell holes, PHR representatives found religious statuary, bibles, and vestments still strewn across the floor. Orthodox churches had also been damaged in Vukovar but were undergoing repairs.

Detention Centers and Camps

Since the spring of 1992, all of the warring factions have operated a variety of detention centers and prison camps throughout the former Yugoslavia. The UN Commission of Experts gathered information on 715 camps but believes that the real number is much higher.[83] Most of these camps are now closed.

To varying degrees, all sides in the wars in the former Yugoslavia have mistreated prisoners of war and civilians held in detention facilities under their control. Prisoners have been summarily executed, tortured, raped, and held in appalling living conditions.[84]

---

[83] *Final Report of the Commission of Experts established Pursuant to Security Council Resolution 780 (1992)*, p. 51.

[84] Article 30 of the Fourth Geneva Convention provides that the International Committee of the Red Cross (ICRC) shall have access to detention camps where "no physical or moral coercion shall be exercised against protected persons, in particular to obtain information from them

PHR has provided medical and forensic expertise to the International Criminal Tribunal for the former Yugoslavia to analyze medical reports and photographic evidence of torture and other abuses in prison camps. PHR has also gathered physical and testimonial evidence on the treatment of detainees in the former Yugoslavia. In October 1993, a PHR forensic team discovered several unmarked graves near an abandoned building once used as a changing room for soccer players in the Croatian village of Pakracka Poljana (see Appendix B). According to UN investigators, a local Croatian army commander used the building as a detention center between October 1991 and April 1992. One former detainee, a Serb, described his treatment at the facility:

> On December 22, 1991, I was arrested in the afternoon around 3 pm in Dereza...The Croatian army had attacked Dereza about 10 am and we were defending against them in the woods and ran out of bullets...They took us to the changing rooms in Pakracka Poljana...I was beaten outside. They used knives, but they didn't use the sharp side. They put water in my rubber boots and made sure they were always full. When I got to Bjelovar prison, my feet were frozen and a lot of skin came off of my feet and legs...They beat me all night at Pakracka Poljana. I was there nine days...On the third day I saw a man killed. It was about 9 am. I could see through a hole in the bricks where the cement was missing. I saw one man with a rubber baton or blackjack. He hit one man and he fell down in a hole that the prisoners dug. They thought it was for a toilet. But it was a grave.

---

or from third parties." Moreover, protected persons must not be exposed to "murder, torture, [or] corporal punishment" (Article 32), nor "punished for an offense he or she has not personally committed" (Article 33).

The PHR team uncovered nineteen bodies buried in shallow graves in a wooded area 200 yards from the alleged detention center. Most of the bodies bore gunshot wounds consistent with execution-style killings, and some of the bodies had their hands tied with rope.[85] This evidence has been turned over to the International Criminal Tribunal.

Among the largest and most notorious detention camps have been the Serb-run facilities in northwestern Bosnia. Serbian military and police opened the camps during the "ethnic cleansing" campaigns in the Prijedor region in May and June 1992. Thousands of Muslim and Croat men, women, and children were held at the camps in deplorable conditions. The Omarska and Keraterm camps in the municipality of Prijedor were closed in August 1992, and most of the prisoners were transferred to the Trnopolje and Manjača camps, which were emptied of prisoners in November and December 1992, respectively.

In most camps in the Prijedor region, prisoners were killed on a daily basis. Sick and wounded prisoners often were buried alive in mass graves along with the bodies of killed prisoners. The camps were overcrowded and highly unsanitary. Rape was also prevalent. Guards killed women who resisted being raped, often in front of other prisoners. Rapes were also committed in the presence of other prisoners. Mothers of young children were raped in front of their children. Young women were separated from older women and taken to special camps where they were raped several times a day. Many of these women later disappeared or were returned to the camps and replaced by other women. Men were castrated or had their sexual organs mutilated.[86]

---

[85] *Final Report of the Commission of Experts Established Pursuant to Security Council Resolution 780 (1992),* Volume V, Annex X.B, p. 55.

[86] Ibid.

Reports indicate that these camps may have been used as detention centers later by Bosnian Serb authorities.

The most notorious of the Bosnian Serb-run camps was at Omarska, an open-pit iron mine north of Banja Luka. Omarska was a death factory. Of the 13,000 people held there, thousands reportedly died of starvation or were killed by Bosnian Serb guards.[87] Many prisoners were jammed into a warehouse packed so tightly that no one could lie down to sleep. Others were held outside in an open pit, without shelter of any kind. There were no toilets or beds, and prisoners were fed like animals.

Bosnian government forces have abused detainees, although not on the scale of the Bosnian Serbs and Croats. One of the worst government-run detention facilities was a former JNA army barracks in the village of Celibici, in central Bosnia-Herzegovina.[88] After the JNA withdrew from the barracks in May 1992, Bosnian government forces assumed control and used the facility to house Serbian prisoners. Former detainees claim that they saw fellow prisoners beaten to death by guards.

The UN Commission on Human Rights reported in February 1993 that conditions in the Celibici camp were deplorable:

> Prisoners were kept in three buildings in the camp. One is reported to have been a ventilation tunnel about 120 centimeters wide, 30 meters long and 2.5 meters high. Air entered through a small glass window in the door and there was no light. Prisoners in the tunnel used a bucket as a toilet

---

[87] R. Gutman, *Witness to Genocide* (New York: Macmillan Publishing Company, 1993), pp. 28-33.

[88] Helsinki Watch, *War Crimes in Bosnia-Herzegovina* (Volume II), pp. 354-366.

but were not allowed to empty it regularly. Thus, as the tunnel inclined, up to ten centimeters of human waste accumulated at the bottom. For the first twenty days, the detainees were not allowed to wash...For the next one and a half months [the detainees] were given stale pieces of bread the size of a matchbox, with some vegetables, three times a day.[89]

Physical and Psychological Effects

History teaches that acts of violence, whether localized-- such as murder or terrorist attack--or more widespread--such as mass killings and war--not only maim or destroy their intended victims but also undermine the emotional stability of survivors and their families and communities.

In the former Yugoslavia, four years of war and massive human rights abuses have physically and psychologically scarred hundreds of thousands of Croats, Muslims, Serbs, and members of other ethnic groups. In Croatia and Bosnia-Herzegovina alone, European community psychologists estimate that 700,000 people suffer from severe psychological trauma and could benefit from professional assistance.[90] However, the number of local professionals is only sufficient to cover less than one percent of those in need of care.

---

[89] United Nations Commission on Human Rights, "Situation of Human Rights in the Territory of the former Yugoslavia submitted by Mr. Tadeusz Mazowiecki, Special Rapporteur," February 10, 1993, p. 18.

[90] I. Agger, S. Vuk, and J. Mimica, *Theory and Practice of Psycho-Social Projects Under War Conditions* (Zagreb: European Community Humanitarian Office, 1995), p. 11.

Mental health professionals have identified seven basic psycho-social stress factors which can undermine the mental well-being of victims of war and human rights abuses:

- Economic hardship
- Social disruption (separation from family, disappearance of family members, downward change in social role)
- Physical/psychological violence
- Ethnic persecution
- Reception at arrival after flight
- Settlement in collective centers or private accommodation
- Uncertainty about future[91]

A 1994 study[92] of 1,754 refugees and internally displaced persons who sought medical care at a clinic in Zagreb, found that sixty-two percent had witnessed combat with all its terror and horror. Ninety-three percent reported the partial or total destruction of their homes; forty-one percent reported that a close family member had been killed; twenty percent reported being subjected to torture; and almost sixty percent felt they were both physically and mentally ill.

First-hand interviews conducted by PHR in 1993, and data from a physician in the Karlovac refugee camp located outside Zagreb, indicate that former prisoners, held in detention camps in the Prijedor region and at the Manjača camp in Banja Luka, have suffered considerable physical and psychiatric after-effects as a result of their treatment in detention. The physician's findings, far from being typical, present a kind of best-case scenario for former prisoners held in these camps for several reasons: first, an ICRC presence had been established in the prison camp some weeks before the physician's study, with a concomitant but hardly

---

[91] See L.T. Arcel, ed., *War Victims, Trauma and Psycho-Social Care* (Zagreb: European Community Humanitarian Office, 1994), p. 13.

[92] Ibid. pp. 17-19.

total decrease in abuse; second, the most unhealthy prisoners were sent by the ICRC to a hospital in Banja Luka; finally, those prisoners medically examined were mostly young men, therefore likely to be the healthiest prisoners in the camp.

Karlovac transit center was administered in 1993 by the ICRC and housed former prison camp detainees and their families. There was a frequent turnover at the camp, since it was intended as a "way station" for refugees headed to permanent homes, often in other countries. Karlovac housed approximately 3,000 refugees. Exact data on the age structure of the Karlovac population was not available to PHR at the time of our investigation, although it appeared that the majority of refugees at Karlovac were between twenty and fifty years old, approximately ten to twenty percent were children, and about ten percent appeared to be over sixty-five years of age.

The building was dilapidated yet structurally intact. Refugees lived in rooms approximately twenty-five by thirty meters, each housing about seventy-five people. While the hallways of the building were unheated, the rooms were furnished with small wooden stoves able to warm the room to about seventy degrees Fahrenheit.

At the time of the PHR investigation in January 1993, medical care was provided on-site in a makeshift examining suite which included two cots. During the day, the center was staffed by two nurses and a physician. After-hours emergencies were transported via ambulance to the local hospital in Karlovac. The center had a small pharmacy with essential drugs. Medications which were not carried by the center were supplied free of charge to the refugees by pharmacies in the town of Karlovac.

The profile of diagnoses seen by the camp physicians was similar in most respects to that seen by a typical United States family practitioner: minor infectious diseases (upper respiratory infections, gastroenteritis) and musculoskeletal aches and pains made up a large percentage of the visits. However, the profile differs in one major respect: a significant number of physician visits were due to physical and psychological sequelae of the trauma inflicted in the prison camps. An internal January 1993 report by a physician (requesting anonymity) who systematically examined 1,611 prisoners released from a north Bosnian prison camp in the fall of 1992, indicates that a large proportion suffered physical abuse in the camps.

The symptoms reported by patients and signs determined by physical exam are presented in Table 1.

TABLE 1

Symptoms and Signs of former Bosnian Serb Prison Camp Detainees

N = 1611

Symptom or Sign	Number	Percent
Sign of physical abuse	790	49 %
Pain	543	34 %
Cough	199	12 %
Anemia	104	6 %
Lice or scabies	59	4 %
Diarrhea	21	1 %
Parasites	14	1 %
Dehydration	4	0.2 %

While this sample represented the healthiest prisoners from a camp which had been watched by the ICRC for three weeks prior to the prisoners' release, approximately two out of five showed scars of physical abuse, and many of them were also otherwise sick or wounded.

The overall findings were grim. About forty percent of the 1,611 persons examined showed scars of physical abuse, and eight percent showed signs of recent physical abuse. The latter group presumably suffered their abuse before the ICRC's arrival, and had yet to heal. (Those who were not victims of abuse were hardly in good health; thirty-four percent reported pain, and six percent were anemic.)

The psychological sequelae were profound. The nursing staff at the Karlovac refugee camp estimated at least one suicide attempt every two weeks, primarily through drug overdose. Assuming a steady camp population of 3,000, the crude cumulative incidence of suicide in the Karlovac camp would be 78 per 1,000 per year. By comparison, a population-based survey of suicide attempts in the United States indicated a crude cumulative incidence of 3 per 1,000 per year in 1989.[93] The cumulative incidence of suicide attempts in Karlovac refugees is thus 26 times higher than in the United States.

The list of scars and psychological sequelae suggest the type of brutality inflicted on Bosnian Serb prison camp inmates: fractures; circular burns or hypopigmentation (consistent with cigarette burns); linear wounds or scars (consistent with knife wounds); contusions, hematuria, bullet scars, dislocation of extremities or mandible, and fracture of teeth.

Many refugees and internally displaced persons, living in camps throughout the former Yugoslavia, require not only medical care but essential medications for chronic conditions, such as medicines for epilepsy and hypertension, insulin for diabetes, digitalis for heart disease, and chemotherapy for cancer. However, these medications are often difficult to obtain and very costly.

---

[93] M. L. Rosenberg and M.A. Fenley, eds., *Violence in America: A Public Health Approach* (New York: Oxford University Press, 1991).

Health care professionals in the former Yugoslavia are particularly concerned about the mental well-being of rape victims. Rape often results in severe and long-lasting psychological after-effects, including persistent fears, avoidance of situations that trigger memories of rape, profound feelings of shame, difficulty remembering events, intrusive thoughts, and difficulty reestablishing intimate relationships.

Rape may be compounded by an unwanted pregnancy or other forms of trauma, such as death of loved ones, loss of home and community, dislocation, and untreated illness. A UN team that investigated reports of rape in the region in 1993 found that, while some rape victims had been able to choose abortions, "others, who lived in rural areas, were held captive, or lived in communities with religious prohibitions, or laws limiting or denying access to abortion, may have had no choice but to bear an unwanted child."[94]

Children have been particularly vulnerable to war-related trauma in the former Yugoslavia. The majority of war-related deaths and injuries of children have resulted from direct shelling, bombardment, and sniper fire on civilians.[95] Some snipers have targeted children. Children have witnessed the killing and rape of family members and friends, the destruction of their homes, schools, and places of worship, and the disintegration of their communities.

Many, if not most children living in the countries of the former Yugoslavia are at risk of mental health problems. Among a random sample of children in Sarajevo, it was shown that more

---

[94] S. Swiss and J.E. Giller, "Rape as a Crime of War: A Medical Perspective," *Journal of the American Medical Association*, p. 614.

[95] Institute of Medicine and National Research Council, *The Impact of War on Child Health in the Countries of the former Yugoslavia* (Washington, D.C: National Academy Press, 1995), p. 43.

than sixty percent of children have suffered psychological trauma.[96] Before the war, suicide was a rare occurrence in Sarajevo; now, there are reports of suicide among both adults and children. A study in the Serbian city of Novi Sad found that refugee children exhibited more problems, including sadness, anxiety, and easy distraction, than non-refugee children of the same age. Eighty-four percent of the refugee children assigned a negative meaning to the word refugee.[97]

---

[96] United Nations Childrens Fund, *A UNICEF Report on War Trauma Among Children in Sarajevo*, Belgrade, February 1, 1994.

[97] Institute of Medicine and National Research Council, *The Impact of War on Child Health in the Countries of the former Yugoslavia*, op. cit., p. 28.

IV. VIOLATIONS OF MEDICAL NEUTRALITY

The Principle of Medical Neutrality

International humanitarian law seeks to protect health professionals, not as doctors, nurses, or medics, and not as individuals, but as medical practitioners. As such, they are protected not because of their credentials but because of the professional services they render to civilians and to the sick and wounded. L.C. Green, a specialist on the laws of war, writes: "The status of the medical profession during war has never been looked at independently, but has always been considered from a functional point of view, that is to say, in regard to the need to protect the wounded."[98]

International humanitarian law extends a special "protected" status to physicians and other health professionals so long as they actively perform medical functions and do not participate as combatants in the conflict. A physician or health worker who undertakes non-medical functions in a field of armed conflict cannot claim the protection of the rules of war. For instance, Dr. Che Guevara, in his political and combatant roles in Bolivia during the 1960s, would have had no claims to any of the protections associated with medical neutrality. Similarly, the Bosnian Serb leader Radovan Karadžić, a psychiatrist, can hardly claim the rights provided to health professionals under the rules of war.

If physicians and health professionals are extended special protection to attend to the sick and wounded during wartime, they

---

[98] L.C. Green, "War Law and the Medical Profession," in *Essays on the Modern Law of War* (Dobbs Ferry, NY: Transnational Publishers, 1988), p. 106.

are also expected to treat all patients, including prisoners of war, in accordance with internationally-recognized tenets of medical ethics.

The Nuremberg trials following World War II had a profound effect on the development of medical ethics. Witness testimony revealed that Nazi physicians had conducted hideous, often fatal, experiments on concentration camp inmates. Among the so-called "tests" were placing prisoners in low-pressure tanks simulating high altitude, immersing them in near-freezing water, or injecting them with live typhus organisms. Although only twenty-three physicians were charged with medical crimes at Nuremberg, the evidence suggested that hundreds of physicians participated in these "experiments."[99]

Disclosures of medical atrocities during the Nuremberg trials prompted the creation of the World Medical Association (WMA) in 1947.[100] Among the first institutional acts of the WMA was the revision of the Hippocratic Oath in 1948 to preclude a repetition of Auschwitz and Buchenwald: "I will not permit consideration of race, religion, nationality, party politics, or social standing to intervene between my duty and my patient."

---

[99] See "Trials of War Criminals Before the Nuremberg Military Tribunals Under Control Council Law #10," Volume 1; (Washington, D.C.: Superintendent of Documents, U.S. Government Printing Office, 1950); Military Tribunal, Case #1, (*United States vs. Carl Brandt, et al.*), October 1946-April 1949, pp. 27-74.

[100] In contrast, the International Military Tribunal for the Far East, which held war crimes trials in Tokyo against twenty-eight Japanese military civilian leaders between May and November 1946, failed to prosecute Japanese military doctors who had performed horrific experiments in a secret germ-warfare factory on the Manchurian Plain. Hundreds of prisoners of war died as a result of the experiments and hundreds more were killed when the Japanese fled the laboratory. Some of the camp commanders were captured by Soviet troops and were later tried in Khabarovsk in December 1949, after the verdicts in the Tokyo trial had been announced.

The following year, the WMA adopted the International Code of Medical Ethics, which contains the precept "Under no circumstances is a doctor permitted to do anything that would weaken the physical or mental resistance of a human being except from strictly therapeutic or prophylactic indications imposed in the interests of his patients."

International humanitarian law draws on standards of medical ethics when dictating the behavior health professionals must follow in times of war. Article 16 of Protocol I refers to the Hippocratic principle of medical confidentiality:[101]

> No person engaged in medical activities shall be compelled to give to anyone belonging either to an adverse Party, or to his own Party except as required by the law of the latter Party, any information concerning the wounded and sick who are, or who have been, under his care, if such information would, in his opinion, prove harmful to the patients concerned or to their families.

Article 11 of Protocol I prohibits the use of

> any medical procedure which is not indicated by the state of health of the person concerned and which is not consistent with generally accepted medical standards, which would be applied under similar medical circumstances to persons who are nationals of the Party conducting the procedure, and who are in no way deprived of liberty.

---

[101] The principle of medical confidentiality takes on added importance in an ethical and religious conflict, as a clear incentive exists for military and political officials to seek group-identifying data regarding sick and wounded from physicians and nurses.

60

International humanitarian law, like codes of medical ethics,[102] maintains that medical care must be provided in a non-discriminatory manner. Article 16 of the Fourth Geneva Convention states:

> Persons engaged in medical activities shall not be compelled to perform acts or to carry out work contrary to the rules of medical ethics, or to other medical rules, designed for the benefit of the wounded and the sick, or to the provisions of the Conventions or of this Protocol, or to refrain from performing acts or carrying out work required by those rules and provisions.

Definitions

The definitions below are compiled from the Geneva Conventions of 1949, Protocol I of 1977, and the laws and customs of war applicable to all the warring factions in the former Yugoslavia.[103]

---

[102] The World Medical Association's "Regulations in Time of Armed Conflict" specifies that in "emergencies, the physician must always give the required care impartially and without consideration of sex, race, nationality, religion, political affiliation or any other similar criterion."

[103] These definitions were compiled by the International Commission on Medical Neutrality. See International Commission on Medical Neutrality, *Violations of Medical Neutrality: El Salvador* (Seattle: International Commission on Medical Neutrality, March 1991), pp. 5-7.

Wounded and Sick

Persons, whether military or civilian, who, because of trauma, disease or other physical or mental disorder or disability, are in need of medical assistance or care, and who refrain from any act of hostility. These terms also cover maternity cases, the newborn and other persons who may be in need of immediate medical assistance or care, such as the infirm, or expectant mothers, and who refrain from any act of hostility. *Protocol I, Article 8 (a)*

"Wounded" and "sick" also include members of the armed forces who have laid down their arms and those placed *hors de combat* by sickness, [or] wounds ... without any adverse distinction founded on race, colour, religion or faith, birth or wealth, or any other similar criteria. *Geneva Conventions, Article 3*

Medical Personnel

Those persons assigned, by a Party to the conflict, exclusively to the medical purposes enumerated under sub-paragraph (e) definition of medical units or to the administration of medical units, or to the operation or administration of medical transports. Such assignments may be either permanent or temporary. The term includes:

(i) medical personnel of a Party to the conflict, whether military or civilian, including those described in the First and Second Convention [i.e. those in the Armed Forces both in the field and at sea] and those assigned to civil defense organizations;

(ii) medical personnel of national Red Cross and Red Crescent societies and other national voluntary aid societies, duly recognized and authorized by a Party to the conflict;

(iii) medical personnel of medical units or medical transports made available to a Party to the conflict for humanitarian purposes:

> (a) by a neutral or other State which is not a party to that conflict;
> (b) by a recognized and authorized aid society of such a State;
> (c) by an impartial international organization;
> *Protocol I, Article 8 (c)*

(iv) personnel informally or formally trained as health promoters, community first aid workers, or relief volunteers, engaged in the delivery of medical services.

Medical Care and Services

The prevention, diagnosis, and treatment of disease and injury.

Medical Units

Establishments and other units, whether military or civilian, organized for medical purposes, namely, the search for, collection, transportation, diagnosis or treatment--including first-aid treatment--of the wounded, sick and shipwrecked, or for the prevention of disease. The term includes, for example, hospitals and other similar units, blood transfusion centers,

63

preventive medicine centers and institutes, medical depots, and the medical and pharmaceutical stores of such units. Medical units may be fixed or mobile, permanent or temporary.
Protocol I, Article 8 (e)

The term also includes humanitarian relief and other organizations which provide medical care as part of their services.

Medical Transportation

The conveyance by land, water, or air of the wounded, sick, shipwrecked, medical personnel, religious personnel, medical equipment or medical supplies, protected by the Conventions and by this Protocol. *Protocol I, Article 8 (f)*

Medical Transports

Any means of transportation, whether military or civilian, permanent or temporary, assigned exclusively to medical transportation and under the control of a competent authority of a Party to the conflict. *Protocol I, Article 8 (g)*

The term also includes transportation used exclusively for medical purposes by relief organizations, health promoters, and other medical personnel.

Permanent and Temporary Medical Personnel, Units, and Transports

Permanent medical personnel, units and transports, mean those assigned exclusively to medical purposes for an indeterminate period. Temporary medical personnel, units and transports, mean those devoted exclusively to medical purposes for limited periods during the whole of such periods. Unless otherwise specified, the terms "medical personnel," "medical units," and "medical transports" cover both permanent and temporary categories.
Protocol I, Article 8 (k)

Classification of Violations of Medical Neutrality

Violations of medical neutrality can be categorized under regional and international law based on the rights of medical personnel to provide care to the sick and wounded, and on the duties of medical personnel to uphold ethical norms during times of war (see Table 2).[104] Appendix C to this report provides a comprehensive set of legal citations from regional and international instruments and case law, which source the rights and responsibilities recognized in international law. The components

---

[104] This classification scheme is derived, in part, from Physicians for Human Rights, *El Salvador: Health Care under Siege, Violations of Medical Neutrality during the Civil Conflict* (Boston: Physicians for Human Rights, 1980); Julia Devin, "Medical Neutrality in International Law and Practice," in G.L. Wackers and C.T.M. Wennekes, eds., *Violations of Medical Neutrality*, op. cit., pp. 104-123; and International Commission on Medical Neutrality, *Violations of Medical Neutrality: El Salvador,* op. cit. It also benefitted by consultation with James Welsh, Amnesty International, International Secretariat, and Jemera Rone, Human Rights Watch. Full annotations, supplied by Jill Guzman, International Human Rights Law Institute, DePaul University College of Law, appear in Appendix C.

of the scheme supply the framework for investigating violations of medical neutrality in the former Yugoslavia.

TABLE 2

CLASSIFICATION OF VIOLATIONS OF MEDICAL NEUTRALITY

A. Abuse of rights guaranteed by medical neutrality

1. Infringements against the sick and wounded, civilians, and medical personnel

   1.1 Killings or disappearances
   1.2 Torture, or cruel, inhuman or degrading treatment
   1.3 Serious harassment impeding medical functions
   1.4 Punishment for treating the sick and wounded, including punishment for upholding medical confidentiality

2. Infringements against medical facilities and services

   2.1 Bombing or shelling of hospitals and clinics
   2.2 Incursions into hospitals
   2.3 Preventing the function of medical services in conflict areas or occupied territories

B. Abuse of responsibilities required by medical neutrality

3. Abuse of medical facilities

   3.1 Use of hospital/clinic/ambulance for military purposes
   3.2 Misuse of medical emblem (red cross, red crescent)

4. Abuse of medical skills

    4.1 Torture, cruel treatment, or interrogation by medical personnel

    4.2 Selective and discriminatory treatment of wounded combatants or civilians on non-medical grounds

    4.3 Medical treatment given according to military instruction rather than clinical indications

    4.4 Breach of medical confidentiality

Torture, Disappearance, and Killing of the Sick and Wounded and Medical Personnel

International humanitarian and human rights law explicitly prohibits torture, or cruel, inhuman and degrading treatment; disappearance; or killing of the sick and wounded and medical personnel. Article 75 of Protocol I of the Fourth Geneva Conventions strictly forbids violence to the life, health, and physical or mental well-being of civilians and prisoners of war. Protocol I also recognizes "the rights of families to know the fate of their relatives."

All sides in the wars in the former Yugoslavia have been guilty of the torture, disappearance, and killing of the sick and wounded and of medical personnel. Torture usually takes place in detention centers or prison camps, but may also occur in abandoned buildings, at the side of the road, or in people's homes. Overcrowding and unsanitary conditions in detention facilities can also constitute cruel, inhuman, or degrading treatment.

• In 1993, former prisoners released from detention centers in Marino Selo and Pakracka Poljana, near Kutina in the

Republic of Croatia, described how their Croatian captors had tortured everyone, including those who were wounded.[105]

• Bosnian Serb forces have been responsible for the mistreatment and killing of combatants who were *hors de combat*, and of civilians held in detention camps in northwestern Bosnia. Several physicians reportedly disappeared from the camps shortly after their arrival.

• PHR is aware of at least one case of a female nurse (who wishes to remain anonymous) who was raped while attending to medical duties. The incident took place in the spring of 1992 in the Brčko Health Center in northern Bosnia. Three soldiers (one of whom was identified as a Bosnian Serb) reportedly overpowered and raped the nurse in the health center. The nurse became pregnant as a result of the rape.

• Bosnian Serb forces reportedly forced patients out of a psychiatric hospital near Sarajevo in the of spring 1992. Military and paramilitary troops reportedly occupied the Hospital Jagomir, a psychiatric center for chronic mental illnesses and alcohol and drug abuse, and allegedly turned patients out into the streets. Several patients eventually turned up at the psychiatric clinic of the Kosevo Hospital in Sarajevo.

• In April 1993, British peacekeeping forces in Bosnia-Herzegovina reported that Bosnian Croat troops were summarily executing Muslims in the Vitez area, and that two of those killed had been physicians. In another instance, two physicians

---

[105] These accounts were collected between October 1992 and February 1993 by an investigations officer with the United Nations Civilian Police (UNCIVPOL) based in UNPA/Sector West. PHR and the International Criminal Tribunal for the former Yugoslavia have copies of the reports.

travelling from Zenica to their work at Travnik hospital were executed in Vitez.[106]

One of the most egregious assaults on the sick and wounded and medical personnel took place during the siege of the Croatian city of Vukovar near the Serbian border in November 1991. According to eyewitnesses, on November 20, 1991, Yugoslav Peoples' Army (JNA) troops and Serb paramilitary forces loaded over 200 lightly-wounded male patients and hospital staff from the Vukovar Hospital onto buses and drove them away. Only seven of the men have been seen alive since then.

The Vukovar massacre and subsequent investigation by the UN Commission of Experts and PHR, coupled with accounts of the atrocities at Bosnian Serb-run detention centers in northwestern Bosnia, helped prompt the UN Security Council to establish an international tribunal to prosecute war criminals in the former Yugoslavia in May 1993.

The Vukovar Massacre

Following Croatia's secession from Yugoslavia in the summer of 1991, the JNA began occupying certain areas of Croatia in conjunction with local Serbian paramilitary groups. Vukovar became the scene of fierce battle between Croatian troops and Serbian irregular forces backed by the JNA. As the Serbs bombarded the city, directly targeting schools, factories, large apartment complexes, cultural monuments, and hospitals, residents hid in a labyrinth of hastily dug fallout shelters underneath the city. In late November 1991, as victorious Serbian troops entered the city, dozens of residents took refuge in the city hospital.

Before the war, the population of the Vukovar municipality, which included the city and surrounding villages,

---

[106] J.F. Burns, "Vicious "Ethnic Cleansing" Infects Croat-Muslim Villages in Bosnia," *New York Times*, April 21, 1993.

was 84,189.[107] But months of relentless Serbian bombing had reduced the city to rubble, leaving 1,798 people known dead and a further 2,500 missing.

The final days of the Vukovar battle were a chaos of violence. Determined to destroy the last vestiges of Croatian resistance, Serbian soldiers went from house to house, searching for combatants who were later killed or sent to concentration camps. Journalists reported seeing Serbian soldiers and militia pulling men in civilian clothes from columns of refugees and shooting them on the spot.[108]

Under the surrender agreements concluded on November 16 and November 19, 1991, the Serbs agreed to let the International Committee of the Red Cross (ICRC) make a roster of the hundreds of wounded and other people who had taken refuge in the Vukovar Hospital. However, early in the morning of November 20, Army Major Veselin Sljivancanin, who was later indicted by the International Criminal Tribunal for the former Yugoslavia, ordered the nurses and doctors to assemble for a meeting. While the medical staff was attending this meeting, JNA and Serb paramilitary soldiers hurriedly removed about 400 men from the hospital. Among those removed were wounded patients, hospital staff, soldiers who had been defending the city, Croatian political activists, and other civilians. Witnesses claim they saw JNA officers and soldiers at the hospital separating some 300 lightly wounded military and civilian males from the other patients and boarding them on several buses. Most of those taken, males

---

[107] In the 1991 census, the composition of the municipality of Vukovar was 43.7% Croat, 37.4% Serb, 2.7% Ruthenian, 1.6% Hungarian, 1.6% Slovac, and smaller percentages of other nationalities. See I. Matos et al, "The Deliberate Preconceived Destruction of the Hospital During the Seizure of Vukovar," in *Croatian Medical Journal*, Volume 33, War Supplement 2, 1992, p. 121.

[108] C. Sudetic, "U.N. Investigating Croats' Grave Site," *New York Times*, November 29, 1992.

between sixteen and sixty years of age, were never seen again.[109]

On the night of November 20, Belgrade television showed footage taken that morning of Army Major Veselin Sljivancanin blocking Red Cross officials from entering the hospital grounds and saying the access road was mined.

By mid-1992, the United Nation's special rapporteur on the former Yugoslavia, Mr. Tadeusz Mazowiecki, was receiving reports from governments and human rights organizations of the existence of dozens of mass graves in the former federation. Some graves were located next to prison camps. Others lay in fields, or along river banks next to villages.

Mazowiecki invited PHR to send a forensic specialist, Dr. Clyde Collins Snow, and a public health expert, Dr. H. Jack Geiger, to accompany a team of human rights investigators to the former Yugoslavia in October 1992.[110] It was during a meeting in Zagreb with the Mothers of Vukovar, a group of Croatian women searching for relatives who had disappeared during the siege of the city, that the two PHR investigators learned about the events at the Vukovar Hospital. Shortly after the meeting, Snow and Geiger interviewed a Croatian soldier in Snow's hotel room in Zagreb. The soldier said that at the time of the siege of Vukovar he had been the commander of a mine-laying unit.

---

[109] In an interview for *Monitor*, an independent Montenegrin magazine, Col. Sljivancanin admits that Serbian troops did evacuate a number of people from the hospital to a place called Ovčara, but claims he turned these people over to prison authorities in Sremska Mitrovica, a Serbian town which houses a major prison facility.

[110] See Annex II, *Report on the Situation of Human Rights in the Territory of the Former Yugoslavia Submitted by Mr. Tadeusz Mazowiecki, Special Rapporteur of the Commission on Human Rights,* E/CN.4/1992/S-1/10, October 27, 1993, pp. 13-14.

The witness was wounded on October 10, 1991 and, after being treated at the Vukovar Hospital, he began making daily trips there to have his bandages changed. The day before Vukovar fell, on November 19, he escorted his parents to the hospital, as he had heard that it was the place where the evacuation was being organized. His parents were evacuated, but he remained at the hospital to be with two of his friends who were being treated for battle wounds.

According to the witness, on the morning of November 20, JNA soldiers forced him and other hospital patients, as well as several male hospital workers, onto buses. At 11 am, the buses, each containing about sixty prisoners and two JNA guards, were driven to the JNA barracks in Vukovar. Three hours later, the buses proceeded to Ovčara, a collective farm several kilometers outside of Vukovar. There the men were transferred to a large building used as a garage for farm equipment and vehicles. While moving from the buses to the building, JNA soldiers and Serbian paramilitaries beat the men with a variety of blunt instruments. The beatings continued for several hours inside the building; at least two men were beaten to death. About seven of the men were released after Serbs who were present intervened on their behalf. These men were driven back to Vukovar.[111]

At about 6 pm that same day, JNA soldiers divided the prisoners into groups of about twenty men. One by one, each group was loaded onto a truck and driven away. At intervals of about twenty minutes, the truck returned empty and another group was loaded onto it.

The witness told Drs. Snow and Geiger that he was put on one of the last vehicles to leave the farm building, an army truck

---

[111] In March 1993, the Commission of Experts and PHR interviewed six of the men who were released from the farm building. The survivors said that they were set free either because they were Serbs taken by mistake or because their captors identified them as neighbors.

with canvas stretched across the back. He sat in the back of the truck, next to the tailgate. Two soldiers sat in the front cab with Kalashnikov AK-47 rifles, but only prisoners were in the back. He recalled that the truck left the building and turned onto a road that leads to Grabovo, a village about three kilometers southeast of Ovčara. Suddenly, the truck made a left turn onto a dirt field road which ran between a cultivated sunflower field on the left and a heavily wooded area on the right.

The witness grew suspicious. "I jumped out and ran," he said. "The truck kept going. As I ran, I heard one short burst of fire and three single shots." Then there was silence.

The following morning, the witness was recaptured and imprisoned. However, his Serbian captors were apparently unaware that he had been one of the patients taken from the Vukovar Hospital. Several months later, he was released in a prisoner exchange and eventually made his way to Zagreb.

In his Zagreb hotel room, Dr. Snow showed the witness a map of the Vukovar area and asked him to mark where he thought his fellow hospital patients had been executed. The man took a pen from his shirt pocket and drew an X on the map. It was at the end of a ravine on the eastern edge of Ovčara.

Three days later, on the morning of October 18, 1992, Dr. Snow and several UNPROFOR civilian police officers drove the six-kilometer stretch from Vukovar to the farming village of Ovčara. Given the witness's estimates of time and distance between the farm buildings, and from the description of the roads used, Dr. Snow figured only one location fit the description: a dirt road turning off the main road just over a kilometer southeast of the cluster of Ovčara farm buildings. The dirt road led to the head of a ravine, where Dr. Snow and his party discovered three young adult male skeletons partially exposed by erosion and animal scavengers. Two of the skeletons bore signs of perimortem trauma (injuries that had taken place around the time of death). Soon after the discovery of the grave, UNPROFOR authorities took immediate action to insure 24-hour security of the site.

On December 17, 1992, at the request of the UN Commission of Experts, a four-member PHR forensic team returned to Ovčara to conduct a preliminary site exploration of the mass grave. The PHR team worked at the Ovčara site for three days and submitted their findings, listed below, to the UN Commission of Experts (see Appendix D):

1. A mass execution took place at the grave site.

2. The grave is a mass grave, containing perhaps as many as 200 bodies.

3. The remote location of the grave suggests that the executioners sought to bury their victims secretly.

4. There is no indication that the grave had been disturbed since the time of execution and interment.

5. The grave appears to be consistent with witness testimony which claims that the site is the place of execution and interment of the patients and medical staff members who disappeared during the evacuation of Vukovar Hospital on November 20, 1991. However, before that determination can be made with scientific certainty, the site will need to be excavated and a number of bodies will need to be identified, using forensic methods and procedures.

6. The fact that two bodies bore necklaces with Roman Catholic crosses -- bearing a small metal plate with the inscription *"BOG I HRVATI"* (God and Croatians) -- suggests that the grave is likely to contain the remains of Croatians.

PHR's repeated efforts to complete the exhumation of the mass grave at Ovčara have been blocked by local Serbian authorities. In October 1993, a PHR forensic team, accompanied by a Dutch military detachment and members of the UN Commission of Experts, were prevented from working by the local Serb commander, who threatened to use force to remove the scientists from the site. In June 1995, the Serbs rebuffed the International Criminal Tribunal when it requested permission to send a PHR team to the site.

On November 9, 1995, the International Criminal Tribunal announced that it had indicted three senior JNA officers for the Vukovar massacre (see Appendix E).[112] The accused are: Mile Mrksic,[113] at the time of the killings a JNA colonel and commander of the Belgrade-based Guards Brigade; Miroslav Radic, a former JNA captain in the Guards Brigade; and Veselin Sljivancanin, at the time a JNA major and a security officer for the Guards Brigade. The officers were not accused of taking part in the actual massacre, but were charged with war crimes and crimes against humanity because they had "command responsibility" for the atrocities carried out by their troops. By May 1996, the three men remained at large, presumably in Serbia or Montenegro.

The indictments are the first handed down for Yugoslav government officials. Thus, President Milošević faces a delicate decision. Refusal to hand over the three men could mean that economic aid, promised under the terms of the peace accords, will

---

[112] Indictment, International Criminal Tribunal for the former Yugoslavia, November 7, 1995, IT/95/13/I, D212-214.

[113] Mile Mrksic, who is now a general in the Yugoslav Peoples' Army (JNA), was sent from Belgrade to command the then Serb-held area of Croatia known as the Krajina in May 1992. In August 1995, when Croatia attacked, he led a hasty evacuation that left close to 200,000 Serbs as refugees.

not be given to Serbia until the officers are arrested and turned over to the International Criminal Tribunal.

Military Attacks on Medical Personnel and Units

Civilians in wartime often take refuge in churches, mosques, or temples. They may also seek shelter in hospitals and other medical facilities. All of these sites, so long as they are not used for military purposes, are protected under international law from military attack. The cruel irony of the wars in the former Yugoslavia is that no building--whether religious, cultural, or medical--has been safe.

International humanitarian law specifically prohibits military attacks on medical personnel and units. The Fourth Geneva Convention specifies in Article 20 that "Persons regularly and solely engaged in the operation and administration of civilian hospitals ... shall be respected and protected." Article 19 also addresses the protection of civilian hospitals, but says that such protection may be forfeited if "they are used to commit, outside their humanitarian duties, acts harmful to the enemy." Military attacks which are considered violations of medical neutrality include:

1. attacks upon medical personnel, or units clearly marked with an easily recognizable medical emblem;

2. continuation of attacks upon unmarked medical personnel or units, after it has become apparent that the object of the attack is a medical unit or medical personnel;

3. failure to provide sufficient warning in the case of an attack upon a medical unit that is also being used for the commission of hostile acts;

4. looting;

5. destruction or closure (whether temporary or permanent) of a medical unit by one of the parties to the conflict;

6. knowing interruption of the supply of food, water, medicines or electricity to medical units.

While all sides in the Yugoslav wars have deliberately shelled or shot at hospitals, health clinics, ambulances and other medical vehicles, and humanitarian relief convoys, the overwhelming number of attacks documented by PHR and other human rights and humanitarian agencies were committed by Bosnian Serb forces. These attacks were intended to terrorize patients, medical personnel, and the civilian population at large. Repeated and systematic attacks on hospitals were carried out to destroy a town's health infrastructure and to force civilians to flee. Examples of military attacks on medical personnel and units in the former Yugoslavia are as follows (also see Appendix G for partial list of health professionals who were killed during the war):

• On May 18, 1992, Bosnian Serb troops fired on an ICRC convoy carrying food and medical relief to Sarajevo. The attack left three ICRC staff members wounded--one of whom, Frederic Maurice, died the next day in a Sarajevo hospital.

The soldiers also destroyed 4.5 tons of medicines and medical supplies.[114] Two days later, the ICRC announced that it was temporarily withdrawing its delegates from Bosnia-Herzegovina. In announcing its decision, the ICRC stated:

the terrible escalation of violence in this strife-torn republic shows no sign of abating ... [and under] these

---

[114] See "Bosnia-Herzegovina: Three ICRC Staff Injured in Sarajevo," ICRC Press Release No. 1715, May 18, 1992, and "Bosnia-Herzegovina: ICRC Delegate Dies in Sarajevo," ICRC Press Release No. 1716, May 19, 1992.

circumstances, when the most basic rights of the victims and especially vulnerable groups are being constantly and deliberately violated, the ICRC is no longer in a position to carry out its humanitarian task.

ICRC delegates returned to Bosnia-Herzegovina in June 1992.[115] By 1995, the ICRC was operating fifteen missions throughout Bosnia-Herzegovina.

• On June 24, 1992, Bosnian Serb troops opened fire on two ambulances in Sarajevo, killing all six occupants. That same day, a third ambulance was attacked with gunfire near a Serbian checkpoint between Dobrinja and the main road to Bosnian government-controlled central Sarajevo. The driver was hit in the thigh, a severely wounded man was hit several times, and a medic was wounded. Journalists later counted 178 bullet holes in the vehicle.[116]

• On July 2, 1992, UN peacekeepers escorted local medical workers to the old Jewish cemetery on a hillside near Sarajevo's city center to remove the remains of seven Muslims--six militiamen and a civilian women--who had been shot by Bosnian Serb troops two weeks before and left there for dead. The medical workers were only able to remove four of the bodies before Serbian sniper fire forced them to leave the cemetery. According to UN officials, on the day the seven were shot, UN troops had observed that the victims still appeared to be alive and in need of urgent medical care. But when UN troops tried to reach the injured they were blocked by Bosnian Serb troops. For

---

[115] "ICRC: Humanitarian Situation in Bosnia-Herzegovina Intolerable," ICRC Press Release No. 1719, May 27, 1992 and "ICRC Returns to Bosnia-Herzegovina," ICRC Communication to the Press No. 92/16, June 24, 1992.

[116] B. Harden, "The Land of Peril for Journalists," *International Herald Tribune*, July 28, 1992.

two weeks, the parents of the seven watched the bodies decompose from the upper floors of nearby buildings.[117]

• In late 1992, several Croatian hospitals were deliberately and repeatedly shelled by JNA and Serbian paramilitary forces. The World Health Organization reported in October that the hospital in Slavonski Brod had suffered "twenty direct hits and many near-misses." The WHO also said the 600-bed hospital in Vinkovci was "subjected to deliberate and persistent attempts to destroy it with heavy weapons," leaving all its windows shattered and its walls ruined at several points.[118] During the siege of Vukovar in November, physicians reported that the city hospital "was shelled every day, sometimes for four hours or more ... We were never warned about attacks. We counted more than fifteen direct hits by airplane bombs from August 25, 1991" until the end of the siege in mid-November.[119] Systematic shelling was also directed at hospitals in Osijek and Sisak, among other places.

• In January 1993 and December 1995, PHR interviewed Dr. Nedim Jaganjac, a Sarajevo physician working with UNICEF, regarding an incident in which his life was threatened while he was in the process of giving medical assistance. Before joining UNICEF, Dr. Jaganjac was a general practitioner working for the Institute for Emergency Medicine who routinely accompanied ambulances to evaluate and treat ill patients in Sarajevo. In late 1992, UN peacekeeping troops escorted him and his team into Ilidza, a Bosnian Serb-controlled suburb of Sarajevo, to evacuate the Institute for Physiatric Medicine. The hospital had been

---

[117] "Terror Not Ended in Sarajevo," *Washington Post*, July 3, 1992.

[118] Donald Acheson, "Croatia: Broken Hospitals, Unbroken Workers," *Lancet*, Vol. 340 (October 3, 1992), p. 843.

[119] "Croatia: War against Vukovar Medical Centre," *Lancet*, Vol. 338 (December 7, 1991), pp. 1447-8.

damaged by a rocket-propelled grenade. After the successful evacuation of sixty-two paraplegic patients and thirty medical personnel from the burning hospital, Dr. Jaganjac returned to negotiate free access to all areas in order to sustain emergency medical service for all citizens. A Bosnian Serb soldier unexpectedly approached him from behind and grabbed Dr. Jaganjac by his hair. The soldier extended the physician's neck sharply and put a knife to his throat is if preparing to slit it. The UN troops immediately levelled their weapons at the soldier, making clear that they would shoot if the physician were harmed. The soldier backed off, "evidently unaccustomed to such UN resolve," Dr. Jaganjac said.

• On January 30, 1993, Dr. Vlado Biljenki, a 59-year-old ophthalmologist, was killed when shrapnel ripped through his operating theater at the Ophthalmological Clinic in Sarajevo.[120]

• In January 1994, a group of health professionals in the Bosnian city of Mostar sent an appeal for help, via facsimile, to medical colleagues and associations around the world. The one-page letter said that the Mostar hospital had become the target of a medical blockade and "constant heavy artillery fire," mostly from Bosnian Croat forces in the western part of the city.

"We are performing operations," the physicians wrote, "without oxygen and sterile materials, frequently under the light of candles and lanterns." In makeshift clinics throughout the city, medical workers were caring for more than 5,000 patients, most of whom were women, children, and old men. "We have been living for eight months in cellars, hungry and thirsty, naked and barefoot, without electricity and fuel, lacking medicaments, sanitary material and medical equipment, in an almost complete media-blockade, forgotten from the rest of the world." That same

---

[120] "Health and Social Consequences of the Aggression in Bosnia and Herzegovina," A Report of the Institute for Public Health of the Republic and Federation of Bosnia and Herzegovina, 1994, p. 29.

month, the last remaining local ICRC employee in Banja Luka, a Bosnian Muslim, was killed by a hand grenade lobbed at him while he was on duty. Shortly thereafter, a Red Cross vehicle was blown up with plastic explosives.[121]

• On April 19, 1994, the UN Special Envoy for the High Commissioner for Refugees complained directly to the Bosnian Serb leader Radovan Karadžić that his forces had shelled civilian areas in Goražde, a Bosnian Muslim enclave fifty-two kilometers south of Sarajevo. The following day, Karadžić declared peace in Goražde. However, two days later, the UN envoy again told Karadzić: "the building where our ICRC and Médecins sans Frontières colleagues are was hit in overnight attacks ... the evidence continues to indicate that these personnel are being deliberately targeted by your force."[122] The UN Special Rapporteur for the former Yugoslavia later charged that Bosnian Serb forces had carried out "deliberate targeting of civilian and highly...vulnerable targets like hospitals, and interference with attempts to bring care to those who were wounded." In response, Bosnian Serb officials claimed that the Bosnian government had used the hospital as a "military command centre," and that there were "machine-gun emplacements on the roof." To that, the Special Rapporteur said, "International observers, with first-hand knowledge of activities at the hospital, have stated that these allegations were entirely unfounded and that the hospital served no military function during the offensive."[123]

---

[121] UNHCR, *Information Notes*, op.cit., No. 2/94 (February 1994), p. 3.

[122] UNHCR, *Information Notes*, op cit., No. 5/94 (May 1994), p. i.

[123] UN Human Rights Commission, *Seventh Periodic Report*, op. cit., (June 10, 1994), p. 2.

- On May 3, 1995, Croatian Serb forces in the region referred to as the Krajina launched a rocket attack on Zagreb.[124] According to the director of Zagreb's Children's Hospital, one rocket landed in the hospital courtyard, scattering hundreds of bomblets. Four patients were injured--three of them seriously. A three-month-old child and two staff members were also wounded and a policeman was killed while trying to gather the bomblets. The attack shattered the hospital's windows, destroyed lab equipment, and damaged an operating theater. About 200 children were evacuated to the basement of the hospital.[125]

Sarajevo

In 1993, the United Nations awarded its human rights prize to the staff of the Kosevo Hospital in Sarajevo. The UN commended the medical workers for their courage in the face of repeated shelling, rocket assaults, and sniper fire directed at the hospital by Bosnian Serb forces. At the time of the award, most of the physician-staffed ambulances had been destroyed and at least half of the hospital's physicians had left the country. Five medical workers had been killed, and ten wounded.[126]

The Kosevo Hospital is the main university hospital for Bosnia-Herzegovina. It is a large facility that has been nearly decimated after three and a half years of war. By early March 1993, a total of 172 mortal shells had struck Kosevo Hospital and its adjoining medical clinics. Among the clinics most affected by

---

[124] R. Cohen, "Rebel Serbs Pound Zagreb for Second Day," *New York Times*, May 4, 1995.

[125] The day after the attack, PHR released a press release calling on governments and the international medical community to condemn the attacks ("Medical Group Calls Attacks on Children's Hospital and Civilians a Crime of War," May 4, 1995).

[126] E.A. Pretto and M. Begovic, "Mission to Sarajevo," *Prehospital and Disaster Medicine*, 1994; 9:S11-S12.

the shelling were the Podhrastovi Clinic, which received 26 hits; Diagnostics and Polyclinic, 13; Traumatology Clinic, 12; Ophthalmology Clinic, 11; and the Central Medical Department, 9.[127] As the hospital compound is within 300 meters of the confrontation line, and visible from Bosnian Serb positions in the hills surrounding Sarajevo, the UN Commission on Human Rights believes "at least some of those impacts must be considered intentional."[128]

One of the most flagrant military attacks on a medical facility took place in Sarajevo on the afternoon and early morning of May 26 and 27, 1992. Bosnian Serb forces at close range repeatedly shelled the Children's Hospital--the central referring hospital for pediatrics in Bosnia-Herzegovina--and the adjoining Obstetric and Gynecologic Hospital. Dr. Esma Zecevic, the fifty-five-year-old chief pediatrician at the Children's Hospital, and president of the Bosnian Pediatric Society, describes what happened:[129]

> On the morning of May 26, 1992, I had an extremely difficult time getting to the hospital because of heavy sniper fire and blockades. The front lines of the Serb forces were by then only about fifty meters from our hospital. When I finally arrived, I found our staff and patients alike were excited and terribly frightened. Those who had been on call could not get home; in all we had six nurses and three physicians. I contacted our territorial defense commander who reassured me

---

[127] PHR received this information from confidential sources.

[128] UN Commission on Human Rights, *Fifth Periodic Report*, op. cit., (November 17, 1993), p. 13.

[129] See E. Zecevic and J. Schaller, "Human Wrongs: A Children's Hospital Destroyed," *Journal of the American Medical Association* 274 (1995):386.

that he considered it unlikely that Serbian forces would bombard us directly because they knew our building was a hospital, and one for children at that. He told us not to be frightened. Nonetheless, we began to move all our patients down as close to the ground floor as possible.

About 4 o'clock we realized our hospital was being directly bombarded. We simply could not believe this at first. We decided quickly that we must evacuate, since there was no safe place for our children. The Obstetric and Gynecologic Hospital was one hundred meters from us, a larger building with a basement that could be used as a shelter...

Our neo-natal ward contained seventeen newborns, mostly prematures from outside Sarajevo. To evacuate these infants we had to remove them from their incubators. Each of us carried two to three babies and ran to reach the basement of the Obstetric and Gynecologic Hospital. Bullets and shells fell all around us as we ran carrying the children. The noise was awful. By the time we could evacuate the thirty-three children, we were exhausted...We finally succeeded in moving all our patients to the basement of the Obstetric and Gynecologic Hospital where we joined their patients (105 mothers and their newborns, seventy-five gynecologic patients, and some neighborhood mothers and children taking refuge in the hospital), and forty-eight staff members. About five minutes after we had left our clinic, a grenade fell on our neo-natal unit, destroying every incubator and incinerating the unit. Had we waited even a few minutes more, all of our babies would have burned alive...

As we huddled in the basement we could hear heavy shelling of the building directly over our heads. When we called for help by way of a shortwave radio we learned that one floor after another was collapsing on top of us. The patients and mothers were screaming and crying. This went on for hours, for an eternity...[In the morning], trucks and cars arrived and we evacuated the patients to [Kosevo Hospital] two kilometers away. As we left, we were still being fired at; fortunately, no one was killed. However, because of the lack of incubators, warmth, and oxygen, nine of our babies died...

Several days after being evacuated to the Kosevo Hospital, pediatric staff returned to the Children's Hospital to retrieve what little equipment had not been destroyed during the shelling. Amid the rubble they discovered that forty-seven years' worth of patient records had been completely destroyed.

Dr. Zecevic nearly lost her life on September 17, 1994. While she was tending to her sick niece in a civilian zone of Sarajevo, her brother's home came under attack. Dr. Zecevic was shot in the arm and chest, the bullet becoming lodged next to her aorta and vena cava. "I worked every day with the bullet in," she told PHR. "I was the only pediatric nephrologist in Sarajevo. I took pain medication every day while I worked." At the time of initial thoracotomy, Sarajevo surgeons deemed an operation to remove the bullet too risky. Dr. Zecevic, through the assistance of past PHR president Dr. Jane Schaller and UNICEF, then travelled to Boston where she was admitted to the New England Medical Center for removal of the bullet. She then returned to Sarajevo where she continues to work at the children's clinic in Kosevo Hospital.

When PHR representatives visited Sarajevo in 1993, they found large parts of Kosevo Hospital to be entirely shot out by sniper fire and shelling.[130] Windows were covered with plastic sheets, and the interior of the hospital was pock-marked with bullets and mortar holes. Physicians and patients were aware of which corridors were in danger from Serbian snipers. During the five days of PHR research in Sarajevo, the shelling of Kosevo Hospital almost never stopped. A physician expressed reluctance to take her son to the hospital to remove shrapnel from his ear because she feared shelling.

Risto Tervahaute, a Finnish expert on low-temperature survival brought in as a WHO consultant, was troubled by conditions in Sarajevo in December 1992. He found that most windows had been shot out, allowing cold air into buildings, including health facilities.[131] This in turn resulted in burst pipes and sewage problems. Central heat was also disabled. Tervahaute helped in the distribution of sleeping bags and instructions on the avoidance of hypothermia. While hypothermia deaths had occurred, they were generally isolated, and in some cases limited to elderly persons in outlying nursing homes. But the Serbian siege could in some cases be traced directly to needless loss of life.

Sarajevo's water system had collapsed by July 1993, with the city's inhabitants receiving under two percent of their normal

---

[130] In the state hospital's cardiology department, PHR found a shortage of many important drugs including streptokinase, urokinase, long-acting nitroglycerin tablets, digitalis products, and ACE inhibitor drugs. As substitutes, they were using heparin and disotyramid, as well as nitroglycerin sublingual tablets and a single ineffective French calcium channel blocker. Surgical success was dependent upon an unreliable supply of antibiotics.

[131] "Six Planes Reach Sarajevo, Ending 3-Week Relief Hiatus," *New York Times*, December 22, 1992.

supply.[132] Electrical and water supply lines run through both government-controlled areas and regions of the city under the control of the Bosnian Serbs, leaving them highly vulnerable to disruption. The UN Special Rapporteur on Human Rights declared in August 1993 that both the Bosnian Serb forces and the Bosnian government were cutting off water and electricity "as a military weapon."[133]

Under these conditions, medical personnel at Kosevo Hospital had to sterilize surgical instruments over a wood-burning stove and wash soiled linens by hand. Surgeons at Dobrinja Hospital frequently carried out operations by candle light. Off-and-on electricity made kidney dialysis treatment unsafe and significantly reduced the number of incubators available for premature babies. Kosevo Hospital reported deaths of patients as life-support equipment failed. Surgeons had to operate by natural light, without defibrillating equipment, sterile gauze, X-rays, or even running water or electricity. Operating theaters resembled conditions at 19th-century battlefronts, with surgeons wearing the same bloodstained gowns for days on end.[134]

The World Health Organization (WHO) provides Sarajevo and other areas of Bosnia-Herzegovina with the bulk of surgical supplies, including surgical kits developed by the Norwegian Army and Red Cross. As of December 1995, there is still a large demand for external fixators for complex fractures which cannot be repaired internally, as well as for drains and colostomy bags. Single-use plastic infusion bags and tubing are reused at least three

---

[132] J.F. Burns, "In Summer, Sarajevo in Worst Shape Since Winter," *New York Times*, July 8, 1993.

[133] Commission on Human Rights, *Third Periodic Report*, op.cit., (26 August, 1993), p. 3.

[134] T.W. Crane, "Five Days in Sarajevo," *Sonoma County Physician*, July 10, 1993, pp. 10-12.

times, until the plastic deteriorates to the point of disintegration.[135] At times, the neurology clinic at Kosevo Hospital has been stretched so thin that most of the moderately severe neurological cases were simply sent home. Multiple sclerosis, Parkinsonism, epilepsy, and muscular dystrophy were usually deemed insufficient grounds for admission.

WHO officials declared in July 1993 that Sarajevo's health situation was the worst in Europe since World War II.[136] The city's ground water was so polluted that there was a great risk of water-borne epidemics. Approximately 200 cases of dysentery had been reported, and typhoid was becoming a problem. After assessing health conditions in Sarajevo in 1993, a team from the U.S. Agency for International Development reported:

> Conditions of public health in Sarajevo are abysmal. Eighty percent of the city's water supply and the sewage treatment plant are under Bosnian Serb control. There is virtually no running water in the city, either potable or non-potable. Security considerations and lack of fuel prevent garbage collection. The solid waste facilities are within the city, but are inoperable due to shelling and damaged, unmaintainable, machinery. Several wells in the eastern end of town provide much of the town's water in January-February. Collecting water entails additional exposure to dangerous sniper fire, though many citizens travel several kilometers per day to do so.[137]

---

[135] Ibid.

[136] World Health Organization, Zagreb Area Office, "Nutrition Report from 1st-31 July, 1993," p. 2.

[137] U.S. Agency for International Development, Humanitarian Assessment Team, Survey Report, op. cit., VI-5.

Some of Sarajevo's suffering has actually been imposed on it by occasional actions of the Bosnian government or Bosnian forces. At the outbreak of the war, the government relied on the Sarajevo underworld to defend the city from Bosnian Serb attacks. These militia forces took their toll on the city's population, especially Bosnian Serbs, by looting and killing. Bosnian government forces have on occasion shelled the Sarajevo airport, the city's primary lifeline for relief supplies. The airport was on a front line with Bosnian Serbs, who also shelled it. The shelling has usually closed the airport for a time, driving up the price of black-market goods that enter the city via routes controlled by Bosnian army commanders and government officials.[138]

On August 28, 1995, a shell fired from Bosnian Serb positions outside the city struck a marketplace, killing thirty-eight people. Some sixty percent of Sarajevo's buildings have been destroyed or severely damaged. Kosevo Hospital still lacks essential medical supplies. In the first two and a half weeks of June 1995, two patients on the wards of the Kosevo Hospital were killed by snipers, two patients were killed during shelling of the infectious disease ward, and two patients fetching water were killed by a shell in front of the hospital.

Bihać

In September 1995, Bosnian government troops, backed by Croatian artillery, broke the siege by Bosnian Serb forces of Bihać, the northwestern capital of Bosnia. For three years, the 50,000 residents of Bihać, almost all Muslim, had been subjected to shelling and sniper fire from Bosnian Serb positions in the hills surrounding the city.

When PHR representatives visited Bihać in October 1995, the city had no industry and almost no commerce. Most public

---

[138] C.G. Boyd, "Making Peace with the Guilty," *Foreign Affairs*, (September/October 1995), pp. 22-38.

services had barely improved since the siege ended. There was little electricity, no fuel for residential heating and scant running water. Many of the city's residents appeared malnourished. For two-thirds of the city's residents, there were no jobs.[139]

At the Bihać Hospital, PHR representatives met with a group of doctors and nurses who described how they coped during the siege. "It was desperate, really desperate," the hospital director, Dr. Bekir Tatlic, said. "In three years, our team of surgeons performed almost 14,000 major surgeries, far too many for a small hospital like ours, even in peacetime. There were days when we needed hundreds of meters of gauze for bandages. And the bandages, we had to wash and reuse them again and again."

During the siege, humanitarian aid only reached the city sporadically. For two years, the hospital served two meals a day, consisting of bean soup and tea. Most hospital workers never received a salary, simply because there were no funds.

At one point during the siege the confrontation line was only 300 meters away from the hospital. Bosnian Serb snipers shot randomly through hospital windows and at patients and hospital workers as they moved from one building to another. On days when sniperfire and shelling were intense, no one left the hospital compound until nightfall.

The Bihać Hospital suffered its worst attack at 5:45 pm on the afternoon of September 22, 1992, when a Howitzer shell burst into the tuberculosis ward. A nurse who survived the blast described what happened:

> It was dinner time. The patients were sitting at one long table, and I was entering the room with their supper. I don't remember how many patients

---

[139] M. O'Connor, "Besieged by Cold and Hunger," *New York Times*, October 19, 1995.

there were but it was less than twenty. Suddenly,
a strong shock wave threw me out of the room.
When I looked back in, I could see the shell had
gone through the floor. Body parts were
everywhere. But I could see there were some
injured patients who were still alive. So I went
back in, to try and save them.

Ten patients died from the shelling. Several others were severely
injured.

Obstruction of Medical and Other Humanitarian Relief

Obstruction of medical and other humanitarian relief and
attacks on relief personnel are prohibited under international law.
Articles 54 and 70(2) of the Fourth Geneva Convention oblige
parties to the conflict to "allow and facilitate rapid and unimpeded
passage of all relief consignments, equipment and personnel" to
civilian populations, "even if such assistance is destined for the
civilian population of the adverse Party." Article 71(2) provides
that the personnel involved in the distribution and delivery of such
assistance "shall be respected and protected."

The obstruction of relief supplies is a "grave breach" of
humanitarian law if it can be shown that the action taken violated
Articles 146 and 147 of the Fourth Geneva Convention by
"wilfully causing great suffering or serious injury or bodily
harm." When medical and relief supplies are disrupted
deliberately in order to cause great suffering and injury to the
civilian population, then a "grave breach" of humanitarian law is
involved. The case becomes stronger if supported by medical
evidence of bodily injury and harm to the health of the affected
population.

Prohibitions against the obstruction of medical and other
humanitarian relief include:

(1) delay or denial of free passage to sick or wounded persons in need of medical attention;

(2) obstruction of the delivery or confiscation of medical equipment and supplies;

(3) obstruction of movement of relief and medical personnel to areas where they are needed; and

(4) disruption of training programs for health workers, and of health education for the civilian population.

Few wars in recent history have tested the resolve of relief workers as have the wars in the former Yugoslavia of the 1990s. With each new effort to block relief supplies, resource-strapped officials have had to weigh the costs in relation to the benefits of continued attempts to provide relief. Addressing the Expanded Steering Committee of the International Conference on Former Yugoslavia in Geneva on February 2, 1994, UN High Commissioner for Refugees Sadako Ogata noted that "the operations of international organizations intent upon humanitarian relief are indeed saving lives [in Bosnia-Herzegovina]." But as a result of denial of access and of ongoing security threats, she said, "it is still falling far short of targeted deliveries of both food and non-food items...there must be a reasonable balance between the risks we take and the energy and money we spend on the one hand, and the needs we actually manage to relieve on the other." She reaffirmed that "the humanitarian needs of the victims remained central." In a chilling query, hinting at the large-scale triage decisions that humanitarian groups confront, the High Commissioner concluded: "Are the risks for a civilian-run relief operation simply not becoming too high? Are more casualties especially among unarmed civilian personnel worth it, if we can hardly reach those who need it most?"[140]

---

[140] UNHCR, *Information Notes*, No. 2/94, op. cit., p. ii.

Although all the warring factions in the former Yugoslavia have obstructed the delivery of medical and other humanitarian relief to civilian populations, Bosnian Serb forces have used humanitarian blockades as a tool of "ethnic cleansing." These blockades have lasted for months and even years, causing extreme physical and mental hardship among the affected civilian population. When the obstruction of relief aid becomes deliberate, widespread, and persistent, such actions are not simply violations of medical neutrality but constitute war crimes and crimes against humanity.

On August 13, 1992, four months after the onset of war in Bosnia-Herzegovina, the UN Security Council authorized peacekeeping troops, who formerly could fire only in self-defense, to "use all necessary means to ensure that humanitarian relief" gets to its destination.[141] However, over the past three years, UN forces have sought to appease the warring factions in Bosnia-Herzegovina rather than use force to ensure the delivery of humanitarian aid. Such submissions have enabled the warring factions--particularly the Bosnia Serb forces--to decide what aid is provided and who will receive it.

Where food needs were concerned, the UNHCR reported in January 1994 that in the preceding month it had delivered less than half of the food requirements for distressed areas of Bosnia-Herzegovina. The delivery of non-food items, including clothing, medicine, and heating fuel, was even further short of the target. The UNHCR reported that while progress was made in the formalities of obtaining clearances for the delivery of such materials by the end of 1993, no significant progress was made in actual deliveries. To explain the failure to deliver such a substantial proportion of humanitarian relief throughout Bosnia-Herzegovina, the UNHCR said:

---

[141] See M. Gorgon, "NATO Seeks Options to Big Troop Deployment for Insuring Delivery of Aid to Bosnia," *New York Times*, August 14, 1992.

Both the Bosnian Croats and the Bosnian Serbs see
the provision of the necessary humanitarian
assistance to the Bosnian government-controlled
areas as against their military and political
interests.

The UNHCR added that "where the Muslim-dominated
government has to make a choice, between military and
humanitarian imperatives, the choice is not in favor of
humanitarian activities."[142]

Bosnian Serb leaders have even flaunted their efforts to
obstruct the delivery of relief. In September 1994, for instance,
the UN High Commissioner for Refugees warned that freedom of
movement for humanitarian aid on the ground and in the air would
be absolutely necessary as Bosnia-Herzegovina braced for the
winter. In response, Radovan Karadžić threatened that "not even
a bird will fly" to those Bosnian government areas dependent upon
access through Serb territory."[143]

The ICRC has repeatedly protested the obstruction of
relief supplies, including clothing, blankets, medical supplies and
medicines to civilian populations in the former Yugoslavia. In
November 1993, after the warring factions in Bosnia-Herzegovina
signed a joint declaration authorizing the ICRC to distribute
humanitarian aid, the agency was only able to distribute forty-six
percent of its planned supplies. The ICRC also reported that it
was only able to fulfill less than half of its delivery objectives for
Bosnia-Herzegovina in preparation for the winter of 1994.[144]

---

[142] UNHCR, *Information Notes*, No. 1/94, op. cit., p. i.

[143] UNHCR, *Information Notes*, No. 9/94, op. cit., p. iv.

[144] International Committee of the Red Cross, "The
Humanitarian Situation in Bosnia-Herzegovina, December 1993," press
release.

Mostar[145]

> "We must not allow the world to
> forget that up to 50,000 people are
> living like rats in cellars without a
> water supply, without electricity,
> without sanitation."

This plea, directed to the UNHCR headquarters in Zagreb,
was written by a UNHCR staff member during the siege of
Mostar in 1994. By then, the Muslim population had been
"cleansed" by Bosnian Croats from the western section of the city
and driven into ghettos in the east. Bosnian Serbs had been
"cleansed" from the town prior to this.

UNHCR responded to the pleas from Mostar, but with
great frustration and limited success. The agency sent food and
medical convoys to both eastern and western Mostar, only to be
effectively blocked by both Bosnian Serb and Croat forces.
Spanish UNPROFOR troops, one of whom was killed by Croatian
fire while delivering medical supplies to a hospital in eastern
Mostar,[146] accompanied the convoys. They were often stopped
by deliberate shelling and sniper fire. While such harassing tactics
often denied access to convoys, more destructive tactics could
completely halt delivery of needed supplies. For example, part of
a mobile hospital (an ambulance, kitchen, and ten tons of
medicine) were finally delivered in February 1994, only to be
totally burned upon arrival. The situation turned worse when

---

[145] Mostar has experienced some of the fiercest fighting in
Bosnia-Herzegovina. Some of the worst battles took place in April and
May 1992, with joint Bosnian Croat paramilitary forces, or Croatian
Defence Council (HVO) and Bosnian Muslim forces on one side, and
Yugoslav Peoples' Army (JNA) and Bosnian Serb militia on the other
side. Later, the HVO turned against the Bosnian Muslims.

[146] C. Sudetic, "Top UN General in Bosnia Warns of a
Withdrawal," *New York Times*, June 2, 1993.

heavy Croatian gunfire prevented the local fire brigade from extinguishing the blaze.[147]

Srebrenica

The siege of Srebrenica in 1993 by Bosnian Serb forces resulted in the deaths of nearly 5,000 civilians.[148] During the peak of the siege, eighty people died in a single week.[149] Louis Gentile, a UNHCR official, said that Serbian shelling was deliberately calculated to kill a maximum number of civilians.[150] John McMillan, another UNHCR spokesman, complained bitterly: "Apparently, in the pathological drive to acquire territory, the Serbs are willing to kill anybody to achieve their ends."[151] He concluded that blocking relief supplies to this Muslim enclave was a tactical component of the drive for territory.

For almost the entire month of April 1993, Bosnian Serb forces surrounding Srebrenica obstructed all convoys of humanitarian supplies.[152] Even after the UN declared the city a "safe area," Bosnian Serb forces refused to let water in or to allow

---

[147] UNHCR, *Information Notes*, No. 3/94 (March 1994), p. ii.

[148] J.F. Burns, "Cease-Fire Seals Serbian Victory in Besieged Bosnian Muslim City," *New York Times*, April 18, 1993.

[149] J.F. Burns, "Muslim Defenders Disarmed, UN Says," *New York Times*, April 22, 1993.

[150] Associated Press, "Serb Shelling of City Sought to Kill Civilians, UN Aide Says," *Boston Globe*, April 15, 1993.

[151] J.F. Burns, "Ending restraint, UN Aides Denounce Serbs for Shelling," *New York Times*, April 14, 1993.

[152] P. Lewis, "Serbs Appear to Step Up Pressure on Bosnia Muslims as New Fighting Rages," *New York Times*, May 5, 1993.

doctors to enter.[153] Residents were reduced to two or three pints of water a day. The water cut-off was no accident: when Canadian UN peacekeepers attempted to repair the water supply, they came under fire and had to retreat.[154]

A UN Security Council mission reached Srebrenica on April 25, 1993. Its leader, Ambassador Diego Aria of Venezuela, criticized the implementation of the UN safe-zone plan. By cutting off electricity and water, he said, Bosnian Serb forces had created a risk of epidemic. The WHO reported that the destruction of the municipal water system meant that people were forced to obtain water from the Jelini River, which received raw sewage from 25,000 inhabitants.[155]

Bosnian Serb forces also kept doctors, including medical personnel with Médecins sans Frontières, from entering the city. As a result, Srebrenica was left with a single doctor for over 40,000 people, of whom some 30,000 were refugees. Srebrenica's inhabitants were exhausted, overcrowded, living in bombed-out buildings, and cooking outdoors.

Dr. Simon Mardell, a British public health physician, accompanied UNPROFOR General Phillipe Morillon on his March 1993 trip to Srebrenica. Dr. Mardell later told PHR that between forty and sixty people were dying daily in Srebrenica from a

---

[153] C. Sudetic, "Serbs Are Poised to Seize Enclave," *New York Times*, May 7, 1993.

[154] Associated Press, "5 Killed in Srebrenica," *New York Times*, May 2, 1993.

[155] World Health Organization, "Visit to Srebrenica: Recommendations," A. Robertson, unpublished, September 1993; quoted in Jonathan Mann, M.D., M.P.H., Ernest Drucker, Ph.D., Daniel Tarantola, M.D., Mary Pat McCabe, B.S., *Bosnia: War and Public Health* (Cambridge: Harvard Einstein Study Group, 1994), p. 11.

combination of Serbian shellfire, privation, pneumonia, and exposure.

One doctor's account of conditions at the main 100-bed hospital in Srebrenica gives a grim sense of the humanitarian consequences of the siege. Dr. Nedret Majkanovic, who had never done more than assist surgeons previously, was the most experienced of a staff that then consisted of six physicians. Dr. Majkanovic and his team carried out some 100 amputations without anesthetics in about eight months. Other patients were fully conscious during some major surgeries. Dr. Majkanovic estimates that up to fifteen percent of 4,000 patients died.

In the early spring of 1993, some twenty to thirty people were dying daily in Srebrenica from pneumonia and other illnesses exacerbated by cold, hunger, and exhaustion. The hospital's task was hugely complicated by lack of supplies of medicine, blood, and bandages. Staff improvised bandages, sometimes from infant diapers that were boiled and reused multiple times. Blood type could not be determined because of lack of lab equipment, so donors from Srebrenica were unable to provide a usable supply for the hospital.

The Bosnian Serb forces finally stormed Srebrenica on the afternoon of July 10, 1995. At the time, there were more than 40,000 people seeking shelter in the city. According to the *New York Times*,[156] a UN officer in the town sent this desperate plea to his superiors in Geneva:

> Urgent urgent urgent. B.S.A. [Bosnian Serb
> Army] is entering the town of Srebrenica. Will
> someone stop this immediately and save these

---

[156] S. Engelberg, T. Weiner, R. Bonner, and J. Perlez, "Srebrenica: The Days of Slaughter," *New York Times*, October 29, 1995.

PHR MASS GRAVE INVESTIGATION AT VUKOVAR

The south side of the hospital building in Vukovar. Yugoslav People's Army (JNA) forces occupied the hospital in mid-November 1991. At that time, the hospital held several hundred civilian and military patients, most of whom had been wounded in the heavy fighting in and around Vukovar during the preceding months. *(Courtesy of Ministry of Health, Republic of Croatia)*

Representative of the International Committee of the Red Cross is denied entry into Vukovar Hospital by JNA paramilitary forces. The ICRC was to monitor the evacuation of Croatian patients from the hospital, as agreed by both sides of the conflict. *(Courtesy of Belgrade TV)*

According to witness testimony, reservists and Yugoslav People's Army (JNA) officers and soldiers took wounded military and civilian patients and male hospital workers on buses, each containing about 60 prisoners and two JNA guards, to the JNA barracks in Vukovar on November 20, 1991. The men were then transferred to a large building used as a garage for farm equipment and vehicles in the farming village of Ovcara (shown) where they were allegedly beaten.

According to witness testimony, trucks left the buildings and traveled to a heavily wooded area near a cultivated sunflower field some 3 km southeast of Ovcara where a mass execution allegedly occurred. The PHR forensic team dug a 1 meter x 7 meter test trench across a 7 meter by 9 meter area to try to determine the size of the grave and its contents.

Markers indicate where clusters of spent 7.62 mm cartridges of the type used in Kalishnikov firearms were found in bushes northwest of the gravesite. No cartridges were found on the northeastern or southern sides of the grave, indicating that a line of fire occurred from one direction near the grave.

Numerous bullet scorings were found on the small acacia trees southeast of the grave, including on one tree just north of the location of two surface skeletons. Bullets also penetrated a rusted vehicle chassis in the area.

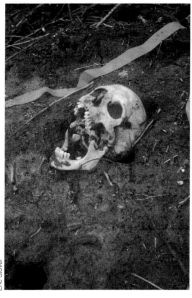

A preliminary inspection of the site revealed three young adult male skeletons partially exposed by erosion and animal scavengers. Two of the skeletons bore signs of perimortem trauma. This skull exhibits two externally-beveled exit wounds on the left cranial vault.

A necklace was found on the first surface skeleton in the grave. It contained a medallion with the inscription, "BOG I HRVATI—God and Croatia"— and a Roman Catholic cross, suggesting that the grave is likely to contain the remains of Croatians.

Jersey recovered from a skeleton exposed at the site. PHR received reports that a Canadian humanitarian group had provided Vukovar Hospital with clothing in 1991.

Forensic scientists conducted a quick analysis of the bones upon location of remains.

State Hospital of Sarajevo
After the siege of Sarajevo began in 1992, this hospital was shelled and hit by sniper fire. Medical services are conducted on the ground floor only.

The Obstetrical & Gynecological Institute (white building on hill) and the Children's Clinic (gray cement building, right) were some 50 yards from the Serb front line during the siege of Sarajevo.

The Children's Clinic of Sarajevo was shelled and destroyed in May 1992. Dr. Esma Zecevic, chief pediatrician, and her staff evacuated seventeen newborns (many removed from their incubators and without supplemental oxygen) and 33 older sick children to the basement of the Obstetrical & Gynecological Institute, 100 meters away. Bullets and shells fell around them as they carried the children. Five minutes after they left the clinic, a grenade fell on the neonatal unit, destroying every incubator and incinerating the unit.

Entryway of the Obstetrical and Gynecological Institute of Sarajevo, September 1994. Dr. Zecevic and her staff and patients from the nearby Children's Clinic took refuge in the basement here along with 105 mothers and their newborns, 75 gynecologic patients, some neighborhood mothers and children, and 48 staff members. There were no lights, no water, and only a few candles. Heavy shelling occurred for hours above their heads. Patients were evacuated to the main university hospital two kilometers away the next morning. Nine of the babies died due to lack of incubators, warmth, and oxygen. 47 years of patient records were destroyed.

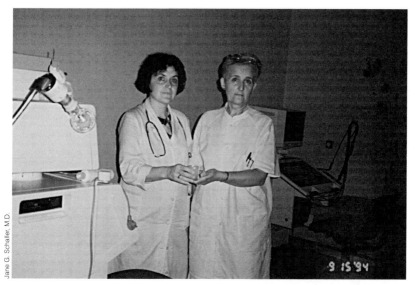

Dr. Zecevic (right) set up the new pediatric clinic at Kosevo Hospital in a ward that had no electricity or windows. In order to continue operating the pediatric service, physicians worked by candlelight. Ultrasound equipment, (background), was rendered useless without electricity.

The hospital staff received meager meals. Many have not received a salary since the beginning of 1994. Many of the children were undernourished and anemic because of food shortages.

Jane G. Schaller, M.D.

Nedim Jaganjac, M.D.,(right), examines the teaching auditorium of the Obstetrical & Gynecological Institute of Sarajevo in September 1994. The auditorium was destroyed when the upper floors of the building collapsed after heavy shelling in May 1992.

Jane G. Schaller, M.D.

SA·291·152

One of the few functioning ambulances at Kosevo Hospital. Bullet holes pierced the windshield. A physician was killed while riding in this vehicle.

people. Thousands of them are gathering around
the hospital. Please help.

Within forty-eight hours, the eastern Bosnian city was overrun,
and what followed in the villages and fields around Srebrenica was
the worst war crime in Europe since World War II: the summary
killing of 6,000 to 8,000 people.

Medical Participation in War Crimes and Crimes Against Humanity

So far, there appears to be no evidence that any of the
warring factions in the former Yugoslavia have systematically used
physicians and other health professionals to carry out war crimes
and crimes against humanity.[157] Nor does it appear that any of
the parties to the conflict have systematically misused the medical
emblem (red cross or red crescent), or used medical facilities or
vehicles for military purposes, although there have been isolated
reports that both Bosnian Serb and Bosnian government forces
have occasionally occupied and operated out of health clinics and
hospitals.

Medical involvement in torture, directly or indirectly, is
strictly forbidden under international humanitarian law and basic

---

[157] Dr. Radovan Karadžić, a psychiatrist by training, has been
indicted by the International Criminal Tribunal for a series of crimes
including acts of genocide. The charges stem from Karadžić's role as a
politician and the leader of the Bosnian Serb forces, and not as a
psychiatrist. However, the possibility exists that the International
Criminal Tribunal could uncover evidence that Karadžić used his training
in human behavior to develop and implement military strategies aimed at
terrorizing and humiliating targeted civilian populations. See D. Silove,
"The Psychiatrist as a Political Leader in War: Does the Medical
Profession Have a Monitoring Role," *Journal of Nervous and Mental
Disease*, Vol. 183, No. 3, 1995, p. 125-126.

tenets of medical ethics. The Principles of Medical Ethics adopted by the UN General Assembly in 1982 state:

> It is a gross contravention of medical ethics as well as an offence under applicable international instruments, for health personnel, particularly physicians, to engage, actively or passively, in acts which constitute participation in, complicity in, incitement, or attempts to commit torture or other cruel, inhuman, or degrading treatment or punishment.[158]

PHR has received reports that medical personnel in the former Yugoslavia have participated in torture and other forms of cruel treatment, or failed to provide proper treatment to detainees, although it appears that such incidents are rare. For instance, Human Rights Watch reported in November 1994 that medical personnel in a hospital in Bosnia-Herzegovina had mistreated a Muslim woman after she gave birth to her first child.[159] On June 6, 1994, twenty-year-old N.A. went to the Bijeljina hospital to deliver her baby. She gave birth without incident but recalls that when the doctor, who is a Bosnian Serb, began stitching her up she felt intense pain and began screaming.

For three months, N.A. continued to feel intense pain and finally went to see doctors at the Tuzla hospital. They discovered that after her delivery, N.A.'s vagina had been stitched with wire,

---

[158] For the text of the Principles of Medical Ethics Relevant to the Role of Health Personnel, Particularly Physicians, in the Protection of Prisoners and Detainees against Torture, and Other Cruel, Inhuman or Degrading Treatment or Punishment, see E. Stover and E.O. Nightingale, *The Breaking of Bodies and Minds: Torture, Psychiatric Abuse, and the Health Professions* (New York: W.H. Freeman and Company, 1985), p. 106.

[159] Human Rights Watch/Helsinki, *Bosnia-Herzegovina: Ethnic Cleansing Continues in Northern Bosnia*, November 1994, pp. 15-16.

and the surgical needle and the wire remained in N.A.'s vagina for three months. According to N.A., Mirko Medan, a doctor in the Bijeljina hospital, had stitched her vagina after her delivery.

After repeated surgeries at the Tuzla hospital, doctors removed about two centimeters of coil, that resembled "a spring used in ball-point pens, and a surgical needle." Human Rights Watch representatives interviewed N.A. and her doctors about the incident and were shown X-rays, as well as the coil and needle removed from N.A.'s vagina. The use of such materials in gynecological surgery is unheard of and clearly harmful to the patient's health.

PHR knows of several incidences of physicians and other health professionals who have risked their own lives to expose human rights abuses or to protect patients and fellow prisoners. The example of Dr. Idriz Merdizic is particularly notable. Detained by Bosnian Serb forces in the summer of 1992, Dr. Merdizic was held in the Trnopolje prison camp near Banja Luka. Since the prison did not provide medical care, Dr. Merdizic and several of his imprisoned colleagues attended to their fellow prisoners. Shortly before his release, Dr. Merdizic was able to secretly hand over to visiting journalists photographs of prisoners who had been tortured. Dr. Merdizic was later released and took refuge in Croatia.[160]

The Practice of Discriminatory Medicine

In the context of medical neutrality, discriminatory practices refer to health professionals giving differential medical care to sick and wounded patients based on non-medical considerations. Discrimination as an abuse of medical neutrality includes provision of substandard medical care to patients based

---

[160] ABC-TV Nightline, "Bosnia: The Hidden Horrors, Part 2," broadcast November 11, 1992.

on political or other non-medical considerations. Equally reprehensible is the refusal to appropriate available resources (e.g., medication, instruments, hospital beds) to wounded or sick patients, or requiring medical personnel to give priority to certain sick or wounded patients, based on political or other non-medical considerations.

The First Protocol to the Fourth Geneva Convention states:

> 1. All the wounded, sick and shipwrecked, to whichever Party they belong, shall be respected and protected.
>
> 2. In all circumstances they shall be treated humanely and shall receive, to the fullest extent practicable and with the least possible delay, the medical care and attention required by their condition. There shall be no distinction among them founded on any grounds other than medical ones.

PHR has received isolated reports of prejudicial treatment and discriminatory abuse by health professionals in the former Yugoslavia. But such complaints stand in sharp contrast to the norm of nondiscrimination that generally prevails among medical personnel from all ethnic groups.

Many patients in the former Yugoslavia have received less than adequate care, but this has been due to war conditions and not necessarily discriminatory medical practices. For instance, the UN Special Rapporteur for Human Rights issued an alert in October 1994 regarding the situation of mentally disabled children and adults in the former federation.[161] "These people are, in some cases, totally neglected," he said. "The spectrum of their needs is very great." The most obvious needs are drugs, including sedatives, clothing, bedding materials and food. The Rapporteur's field staff observed examples of "medical staff...forced to resort to tying the patients up for control because of the lack of suitable drugs."[162]

PHR is concerned about a report by the U.S. Agency for International Development which states that an agency assessment team found examples of unequal treatment among patients in Croatia. The team heard expressions of governmental concerns that the state could no longer afford to continue to offer health care to refugees beyond emergency services and vaccinations. In response to an infusion of new money from UNHCR, the government formally reversed the policy. Even so, the team later heard reports that Bosnian Muslims were discriminated against and were either put at the end of the line or not admitted at all. The team reported seeing wounded Bosnian Muslims who were denied entrance to hospitals in Zagreb. Notwithstanding that observation, they reported that they "also toured the Children's Hospital, where the same loving care was given to Croats, Muslims, and Serbs alike."[163] The Director of Surgery of the 500-bed hospital in Travnik told PHR, in November 1995, that his hospital had taken great pride in its nondiscriminatory treatment of all patients, including injured Bosnian and Serb soldiers alike.

---

[161] A UN official told PHR, on condition of anonymity, that one of "the worst human rights problems in many areas of the former Yugoslavia involves the inhumane warehousing of psychiatric patients."

[162] UN Commission on Human Rights, *Sixth Periodic Report*, op. cit., February 21, 1994.

[163] "Assistance for Victims of Atrocities in Croatia and Bosnia-Herzegovina," unpublished, U.S. Agency for International Development, 1993, p. 28.

A PHR team visited Zvornik Hospital in January 1993 and reported several Muslim children being cared for by Serbian medical staff. Previous local newspaper reports had claimed that these children were being maltreated.

PHR is concerned at reports that some doctors in the former Yugoslavia have placed partisanship above their duty to provide impartial care to all wounded and sick persons. In January 1993, PHR took testimonies from Bosnian refugees in a Croat refugee camp who reported that a military physician at the Bosnian Serb-controlled Batkovici detention camp, near Bijeljina, often abused them or refused health care to patients based on their ethnicity. Witnesses said they only knew the doctor's first name: Zeljko. He told one Muslim patient: "You did not come here to be cured, to have treatment, but to die." Then, turning to nearby Serbian soldiers and referring to the prisoner's legs, he told them, "just break, I will heal."

A Bosnian Croat held at the same camp tried to get treatment from the same doctor for his dislocated shoulder. The doctor called the man "an Ustashe son of a bitch" and left the room. Fifteen days later, the patient tried again; this time, the doctor struck him across the body and said, "You son of a bitch, I have already told you, you do not need treatment."

"Ethnic cleansing" throughout the former Yugoslavia has nurtured discrimination at almost every level of society, including in the ranks of medical professionals. For example, in 1992, the *Croatian Medical Journal* published a racist tract by one Eduard Klain, of the Zagreb University School of Medicine. Klain writes of the Serbs as having "the complex of inferiority, because they are aware of their lower level of civilization and culture," and describes the Bosnian Muslims as "an undistinguished ethnic group." By way of contrast, he writes that the Croats have developed a society built on "labor, dialogue, obedience, expectance [sic] of understanding and justice."[164]

In a grotesque misuse of psychiatry, and advancing no evidence, the article continues:

> In the Croats, the group regression is closer to the depressive position in the development of a personality, which is characterized by the feeling of guilt which, among other things, manifests in their need to pray to God. In Serbs, the group regression is more frequently at the level of the schizo-paranoid position in the development of a personality, accompanied by complete destructiveness and irrationality brought along by this phase.[165]

Such writing has absolutely no place in medical and scientific literature.

There are other examples of the politicization of the medical profession. From February to May 1994, a media campaign was directed at Serb medical professionals working at Rovinj Hospital in the Republic of Croatia. The wounded Croatian soldiers treated in the hospital accused the non-Croat staff, including doctors, of abusing, mistreating, and provoking them. The chairman of an ad hoc parliamentary commission, established to verify the allegations, was the first to question the validity of the accused doctors' certificates of citizenship. When interviewed, the Croatian Minister of Health, Mr. Andrija Hebrang, stated his belief that the conflict was caused by the presence of Serbian staff in a Croatian hospital. The conflict, he

---

[164] E. Klain, "Yugoslavia as a Group," *Croatian Medical Journal*, Vol. 33 (War Supplement 1, 1992), pp. 5-6.

[165] Ibid., p. 5.

said, could not be resolved, so long as "our invalids and those staff people" remained living together in the hospital.[166] However, after field staff of the UN Special Rapporteur gathered credible evidence indicating that accusations against the Serbian staff were false, the issue quickly disappeared from the public agenda.[167]

PHR is concerned about an incident in August 1995 in which a Croatian physician allegedly refused to treat an elderly Serbian patient. The man, an 82-year-old Serb named Jovanovic Branko, chose to remain in his village of Budici in the area known as the Krajina after Croatian troops invaded the region in August 1995. More than 150,000 Serbs fled the Krajina before the advancing troops, but 3,000 remained--those too old or too feeble to flee, or simply unwilling to leave their homes. In late August, a UN patrol found Branko lying in his excrement, suffering from dehydration and malnourishment. UN personnel made repeated pleas to the hospital nearest his village, to treat him. However, the Croatian doctor in charge refused to admit him.[168]

Whether in times of peace or war, physicians and health professionals are strictly bound by medical ethics not to practice discriminatory medicine. As historian L.C. Green has observed, it is the doctor's task, as a professional, to treat the sick and wounded in the same manner at all times. "If it be said that by doing so he runs the risk of punishment or death, it might be pointed out that during an epidemic, his life is also at risk, but this does not seem to inhibit him."[169]

---

[166] Interview in *Novi List*, February 24, 1994.

[167] UN Commission on Human Rights, *Ninth Periodic Report*, op. cit., (October 31, 1994), p. 5.

[168] R. Bonner, "The Abandoned: Elderly Serbs in Region Retaken by Croatia," *New York Times*, December 12, 1995.

[169] L.C. Green, *Essays on the Modern Law of War* op. cit., p. 134.

V. CONCLUSIONS AND RECOMMENDATIONS

Human Rights and Humanitarian Law

Armed conflicts, marked by appalling brutality inflicted on civilians, raged in the territory of the former Yugoslavia from 1991 until late 1995. All parties to the wars have ignored the most basic safeguards intended to protect civilians and medical facilities. The indiscriminate use of force by all sides has caused excessive collateral damage and loss of civilian life.

Many of the abuses committed in the former Yugoslavia constitute "grave breaches" of international humanitarian law, or war crimes. All sides are guilty of holding civilians hostage; mistreating prisoners in detention; forcibly displacing hundreds of thousands of people; and looting and burning homes, businesses, and churches. Especially egregious was the behavior of Croatian troops during the Croatian army offensive into the area known as the Krajina beginning on August 4, 1995. During that offensive, hundreds of thousands of people were displaced. In implementing a brutal scorched-earth policy, Croatian troops murdered Serb civilians--most of them elderly--systematically burned homes and buildings,and looted property.[170]

While all parties are guilty of violations of human rights and humanitarian law, Bosnian Serb forces have systematically implemented a policy of "ethnic cleansing" throughout Serbian-occupied areas of Bosnia-Herzegovina. This policy has resulted in the summary execution, disappearance, arbitrary detention, deportation,and forced displacement of hundreds of thousands of people, on the basis of their religion or nationality. "Ethnic

---

[170] Amnesty International, "Croatia: Human Rights Violations in the Krajina," News Service 186/95, September 29, 1995, AI Index EUR 64/08/95.

cleansing" in some areas, particularly in Srebrenica and the Prijedor region in Bosnia, constitute acts of genocide, which is one of the most heinous crimes known to humankind. The international community has a moral and legal duty to prevent genocide and to see that its instigators and those responsible for parallel war crimes and crimes against humanity are brought to justice.[171]

- Physicians for Human Rights (PHR) calls on the parties to the conflict in the former Yugoslavia to discipline or punish those responsible for violations of human rights and humanitarian law, including violations of medical neutrality. Disciplinary measures taken against individual offenders should be made public. The warring factions should cooperate fully with the International Criminal Tribunal for the former Yugoslavia, which holds criminal jurisdiction over war crimes committed in the former federation since 1991. Moreover, the parties to the Dayton agreement are obliged to honor and not to hinder the objectives of the International Criminal Tribunal as arrests are made of those indicted for war crimes.

- The lifting of sanctions against the Serbian govern-ment should be strictly linked to the following: full cooperation with the investigation and extradition of suspected war criminals; release of all prisoners; the closing of all forced labor camps; guarantee of

---

[171] Article VIII of the Convention on the Prevention and Punishment of the Crime of Genocide provides: "Any Contracting Party may call upon the competent organs of the United Nations to take such action under the Charter of the United Nations as they consider appropriate for the prevention and suppression of acts of genocide or any of the other acts enumerated in Article III." See Appendix F.

the right to return for displaced civilians, as well as the right to remain; and full access for humanitarian and human rights groups as outlined in the Dayton accords.

In its maintenance or reimposition of sanctions, the United Nations must ensure that the humanitarian exemptions for food and medicine are upheld. As it has in the past, PHR urges the United Nations to consider imposing sanctions that are specifically targeted to affect directly those most responsible for violations of international agreements.

- The major powers, and particularly the U.S. government, should publicly name the senior political and military leaders who have presided over atrocities in the former Yugoslavia. Details of their crimes should be made public and provided to the International Criminal Tribunal. The major powers, and particularly the U.S. government, should also disclose all available information, including intelligence reports, of atrocities committed in the former Yugoslavia.[172] In addition, the United States and other governments should disclose any information that might implicate the Serbian government in supplying, assisting or directing Bosnian Serb forces.

- Given reports that Bosnian Serb forces may have executed thousands of Muslim men from Srebrenica and Žepa, the United Nations and individual

---

[172] On November 9, 1995, Reuters News Agency reported that U.S. Department of State spokesman Nicholas Burns had pledged "100 percent cooperation" in supplying relevant U.S. intelligence data to the International Criminal Tribunal. See "U.S. will supply data to war crimes tribunal," *Boston Globe*, November 9, 1995.

governments should demand that the Bosnian Serbs give the International Criminal Tribunal and international humanitarian and human rights organizations immediate access to all detainees being held by Bosnian Serb forces in the region. The International Criminal Tribunal should also have immediate access to alleged execution sites in the Srebrenica area, namely Nova Kasaba-Konjevic Polje (Saldrumica), Kravica, Rasica Gai, Zabrde, Karakaj, and Bratunac.[173] The NATO-led multinational Implementation Force (IFOR) and the civilian International Police Task Force (IPTF) should provide security and logistical support to International Criminal Tribunal staff investigating alleged war crimes in Bosnia-Herzegovina. **This should include landmine detection and clearance, as well as round-the-clock guarding of sites selected by the ICTY for investigation, and security escort for the equipment needed for the scientific investigation of mass graves.**

- IFOR should use decisive military action to stop any future massacres of civilians in Bosnia-Herzegovina. In addition, IFOR should use military force to prevent interference with the free movement of civilians, refugees, and displaced persons and to respond appropriately to violence against civilians. IFOR should have the authority to arrest any indicted war criminals it encounters or who interfere with its mission. Furthermore, no member of IFOR or other international staff should

---

[173] United Nations Security Council, *Report of the Secretary-General Pursuant to Security Council Resolution 1019 (1995) on Violations of International Humanitarian Law in the Areas of Srebrenica, Žepa, Banja Luka and Sanski Most*, November 27, 1995, S/1995/988, p. 3.

have any association with indicted war criminals
other than to arrest them.

International Criminal Tribunal for the former Yugoslavia

Besides the obvious goal of establishing justice, trials of
war criminals can contribute to the rehabilitation of victims of past
abuses and of society itself. By laying bare the truth about past
abuses and condemning them publicly, prosecutions can deter
future offenders and prepare the public to withstand the temptation
or pressures to comply with, or acquiesce to, state-sponsored
violence. Trials often take place at a time when societies are
examining their basic values and can have a cathartic effect on
victims and society at large. Trials also help foster respect for
democratic institutions by demonstrating that no individual--
whether a foot soldier or high government official--is above the
law.

Nowhere in the world is the need to reaffirm the rule of
law and restore justice more pressing than in the former
Yugoslavia and Rwanda.[174] In both countries, the cycle of ethnic
violence and retribution is unlikely to end unless, at a minimum,
trials can restore confidence that justice can be achieved in a lawful
form. By establishing individual guilt, trials will help dispel the
notion of collective blame for genocide and war crimes.

In the former Yugoslavia, an international tribunal is
preferable to ad hoc trials held sporadically in whatever countries
within the region the accused happen to surface. Absent a change

---

[174] After a Hutu-led slaughter claimed the lives of hundreds of
thousands of people in Rwanda between April and July 1994, the UN
Security Council established an international tribunal to prosecute war
crimes and acts of genocide in that country. PHR is assisting the
International Criminal Tribunal in its investigation of mass graves
throughout Rwanda.

111

in regime, the several governments that have carried out atrocities in the former Yugoslavia can hardly be expected to prosecute vigorously those responsible.

Since 1992, the International Criminal Tribunal has been investigating reports of individual criminality associated with war crimes committed since the outbreak of the Yugoslav war in 1991. By May 1996, the International Criminal Tribunal had indicted fifty-seven people, including Radovan Karadžić and General Ratko Mladić, the president and military commander respectively of the Bosnian Serbs.

PHR believes that the creation of the International Criminal Tribunal provides an historic opportunity to demonstrate that genocide, war crimes, and crimes against humanity cannot be committed with impunity. The International Criminal Tribunal promises justice for victims and their families, deterrence against further abuse, and a basis for eventual peace and reconciliation, by establishing individual accountability and therefore avoiding the kind of collective condemnation that only nourishes further ethnic resentment and violence. Moreover, PHR does not believe a peace will ever last in the former Yugoslavia, unless respect for international law and justice is made integral to the negotiation, content, and implementation of a peace agreement.

Since 1992, PHR has provided the UN Commission of Experts, and now the International Criminal Tribunal, with medical, statistical, and forensic expertise. PHR has sent several forensic teams to Croatia and Bosnia to conduct medicolegal investigations of mass graves. These investigations have provided the International Criminal Tribunal with physical evidence of mass killings of civilians and led to the indictment of suspected war criminals.

- The United Nations and individual governments must insist that the International Criminal Tribunal should be free to follow wherever the evidence leads.

- The United Nations should impose or keep in place sanctions and other penalties against any parties to the conflict that refuse to cooperate with the International Criminal Tribunal. In implementing sanctions, the United Nations should make every effort to ensure that the most vulnerable civilians do not suffer undue harm as a result.

- The United Nations and individual governments must recognize that the first step towards lasting peace and reconciliation in the former Yugoslavia is the restoration of justice and the rule of law. To this end, the United Nations and individual governments should increase their financial and diplomatic support of the International Criminal Tribunal.

Violations of Medical Neutrality

In the years after World War II, the former Yugoslavia developed a comprehensive health care system. Its universities and technical schools trained a core of health professionals who generally provided care without regard to religion, ethnicity, or politics. The Yugoslav government became a party to most major international human rights and humanitarian agreements. In 1991, as the former federation began to disintegrate, its five successor states--Croatia, Slovenia, Bosnia-Herzegovina, Serbia, and Montenegro--pledged to abide by the same international standards.

Since the outbreak of war in the former Yugoslavia in 1991, massive human rights abuses have severely eroded respect for medical neutrality in the former Yugoslavia. All sides in the conflict have flagrantly disregarded the rule of proportionality, which holds that civilian casualties and damage to civilian objects should not be out of proportion to the military advantages anticipated. Hospitals and clinics in or near conflict zones have been deliberately and often repeatedly attacked. Patients and medical staff have been shot by snipers and, in at least one case, forcibly removed from hospital wards and summarily executed. Ambulances and other medical vehicles have been the target of mortar and sniper fire. Relief convoys carrying medical supplies have been shelled or prevented from reaching towns and cities under siege.

In some instances, the warring factions, particularly the Bosnian Serbs, have obstructed the delivery of humanitarian aid to civilians, or have allowed relief supplies to pass through check points only after they have confiscated a percentage of foods and medicines. Bosnian Serb forces have blockaded the delivery of relief aid in an effort to starve, and thereby force, the besieged population to flee or surrender. None of these actions have served a military purpose other than to terrorize the civilian population and destroy its medical infrastructure.

PHR is concerned that the mandates of the UN protection and peacekeeping operations in the former Yugoslavia and elsewhere have never contained specific language charging the UN civilian and military personnel with the task of safeguarding medical neutrality.

PHR is concerned that some physicians and their professional associations in the former Yugoslavia have placed partisanship above their duty to provide care to all wounded and sick persons. PHR is particularly appalled by a racist tract which appeared in the *Croatian Medical Journal* in 1992. The article, which presented no medical or scientific evidence to support its claims, directed racial slurs at Serbs and Muslims.

- The United Nations, as a matter of policy, should include specific language on safeguarding medical neutrality in its protection and peacekeeping mandates. With proper monitoring systems in place, the United Nations and NATO forces could watch large troop deployments and routinely warn commanders of their obligations under international

114

law to protect civilians and medical facilities. When violations of medical neutrality occur, UN officials should issue public condemnations and demand that those responsible be disciplined or prosecuted for war crimes.

- Medical associations in the former Yugoslavia should ensure that their members strictly adhere to the ethical duties and obligations set forth in the "Regulations in Time of Armed Conflict," adopted by the World Medical Association in 1956 (edited and amended in 1957 and 1983). Article 4 provides that "the physician must always give the required care impartially and without consideration of sex, race, nationality, religion, political affiliation or any other similar criterion. Such medical assistance must be continued for as long as necessary and practicable." Medical associations in the region should also prevent the publication in professional journals of articles and commentary that subscribe to or promote ethnic or religious hatred.

International Medical Community

In the past four years, hundreds of foreign health professionals have served as volunteers in besieged hospitals and clinics throughout the former Yugoslavia. Physicians in several countries have provided free medical care to emigres who have required specialized care for war-related injuries. Others have organized events to raise funds to send medicines and supplies to the former federation.

A few medical organizations have sponsored workshops and symposia and invited medical colleagues from the five independent Balkan states. The Institute of Medicine of the National Academy of Sciences convened a highly successful meeting in March 1994.[175] The meeting, which was held in Trieste, Italy, brought together nineteen pediatricians from Bosnia-Herzegovina, Croatia, Macedonia, Slovenia, and Serbia, and eleven pediatricians from the rest of Europe and North America. Among the workshop's recommendations was a call for medical associations to take a more active role in supporting their colleagues who continue to practice medicine during armed conflicts.

PHR has found that many physicians and health professionals misunderstand what is meant by the term "medical neutrality." Does "neutrality" mean to suggest that military medical personnel should not take sides in a conflict? Such a notion, of course, would be absurd: medical personnel cannot shed their nationalities. However, the term does suggest that military medical personnel, like their civilian colleagues, must provide medical care impartially and without discrimination. Similarly, the term implies that medical objects, such as hospitals and ambulances, shall be recognized as neutral, and as such, protected and respected by the belligerents as long as they accommodate the wounded and sick. Neutrality, in other words, means that medical personnel and objects are entitled to respect and protection on the part of belligerents by virtue of their functions, not because of some inherent right.

PHR believes that medical, nursing, and public health associations worldwide, and particularly the World Medical Association (WMA) and the International Council of Nurses (ICN), must find effective ways of responding to the political, ethical, and moral dimensions of war. It is not enough simply to provide humanitarian relief; we must also develop strategies to support beleaguered colleagues and their patients, publicly condemn violations of medical neutrality when they occur, and educate

---

[175] Institute of Medicine and National Research Council, *The Impact of War on Child Health in the Countries of the former Yugoslavia*, op. cit.

civilian and military officials about the duties and responsibilities of medical personnel and the basic legal safeguards intended to protect civilians and medical facilities in times of war.

- PHR calls on national medical, nursing, and public health associations, to review their procedures for sanctioning health professionals who fail to discharge their responsibilities in conformity with the standards of medical neutrality set forth in international codes of medical ethics and human rights and humanitarian law. National and international medical and health associations should protest vigorously to offending governments when they violate standards of medical neutrality.

- PHR urges international medical, health, and scientific organizations, such as the United Nations Scientific, Educational and Cultural Organization (UNESCO), the World Health Association (WHO), the World Medical Association (WMA), and the International Council of Nurses (ICN) to work with international human rights and humanitarian organizations to develop and implement effective measures for protecting health professionals and their patients in wartime. Such measures should include the creation of standardized complaint procedures[176] which would enable individuals and institutions to report violations of medical neutrality when they occur. These international organizations should develop educational and training programs

---

[176] See S. Lewis-Anthony, "Treaty-Based Procedures for Making Human Rights Complaints within the UN System," and N.S. Rodley, "United Nations Non-Treaty Procedures for Dealing with Human Rights Violations," in H. Hannum (ed.), *Guide to International Human Rights Practice* (Philadelphia: University of Pennsylvania Press, 2nd edition, 1992).

on international humanitarian and human rights law, similar to those developed by the International Committee of the Red Cross (ICRC).

- In addition to complaint procedures and education programs, international medical, health, and scientific organizations must take a proactive stance to protect colleagues and their patients at the onset of conflicts. These organizations should develop the capacity to conduct rapid assessments at the onset of armed conflicts to pinpoint vulnerable populations and medical facilities. During these assessments, they should meet with military and civilian officials of all parties to the conflict and insist that they respect international humanitarian and human rights law. These organizations should also create a rapid-response network, which will activate national associations worldwide to protest blatant violations of medical neutrality soon after they occur.

- PHR encourages health professionals worldwide to establish "correspondence networks" with their colleagues in the former Yugoslavia and elsewhere.[177] Similar "sister hospital" projects should be established between hospitals and their counterparts in war zones. These networks could provide moral and material support to colleagues and medical facilities at risk, as well as advocate for their protection from military attack.

---

[177] A similar network was established by the Federation of American Scientists during the 1989 demonstrations for democracy and human rights in Tiananmen Square.

- Education and training programs in medicine and public health should include at least one course on international humanitarian law and the duties and responsibilities of medical personnel in wartime.

Appendix A

Rape as a Crime of War

A Medical Perspective

Shana Swiss, MD, Joan E. Giller, MA, MB, MRCOG

Although widespread, rape of women has been an underreported aspect of military conflict until recently. The current war in the former Yugoslavia has focused attention on the use of rape as a deliberate strategy to undermine community bonds and weaken resistance to aggression. In addition to providing treatment for individual survivors, the medical community has an important role to play in investigating and documenting incidents of rape. Such documentation can help to establish the magnitude of rape in war and hold perpetrators accountable. Since rape in war affects not only the individual but also the family and community to which the survivor belongs, the restoration of social and community bonds is central to the process of healing and must be addressed within the specific cultural setting.

(JAMA. 1993;270:612-615)

WRITTEN accounts of rape of women during war date back to ancient Greece.[1] The abduction of Helen of Troy and the rape of the Sabine women are archetypal in Western culture, so much so that their human tragedy is obscured. Despite the fact that rape has always been part of war, little is known about its scale, the circumstances that provoke or aggravate it, or how to prevent it. We know even less about how women heal after the trauma of rape in war and how rape affects the communities in which they live.

Only recently, with the media focus on allegations of widespread rape in the former Yugoslavia, has there been a significant increase in public awareness and support for measures that respond to the trauma and crime of rape in war. A number of agencies, including the United Nations (UN), have begun to develop methods to document the scale of rape in the former Yugoslavia, collect individual testimonies, and provide humanitarian assistance to the survivors of rape in war.

Health care professionals can support individual and community healing from rape and other war-related trauma. We examine herein some of the medical sequelae and human rights issues that surround the crime of rape in war and the role that health care professionals can play in treating individual survivors as well as in collecting and analyzing evidence of these violations.

THE SCALE OF RAPE DURING WAR

Compared with the civilian casualty rate in World War I, an estimated 90% of war casualties in 1990 were civilians,[2] many of whom were women and children. This dramatic change is in part the result of deliberate and systematic violence against whole populations in wars increasingly waged between ethnic groups, as in the former Yugoslavia.

Many hundreds of thousands of women have been raped in wars in this century alone.[1] The following examples give some indication of the scope of the problem:

1. In Korea, recent reports estimate that in World War II, Japanese soldiers abducted between 100 000 and 200 000 Asian women, mostly Korean, and sent them to the front lines, where they were forced into sexual slavery.[3]

2. In Bangladesh, estimates of the number of women raped during the country's 9-month war for independence in 1971 range from 250 000 to 400 000, and these rapes led to an estimated 25 000 pregnancies, according to International Planned Parenthood.[1]

3. In Liberia, health care personnel estimate that large numbers of women and girls have been survivors of sexual coercion and rape during the country's ongoing civil war.[4-6]

4. In Southeast Asia, the UN High Commissioner for Refugees reported that 39% of Vietnamese boat women between the ages of 11 and 40 years were abducted and/or raped at sea in 1985.[7]

5. In Uganda, a village health worker reported that approximately 70% of the women in her community in the Luwero triangle had been raped by soldiers in the early 1980s.[8] Many of the survivors were assaulted by as many as 10 soldiers in a single episode of gang rape.[9]

RAPE AS A STRATEGY OF WAR

The common occurrence of sexual violence and rape of women and girls during detention, torture, and war has previously been documented.[10] In war, rape is an assault on both the individual and her family and community. As well as an attempt to dominate, humiliate, and control behavior,[11] rape in war can also be

From Physicians for Human Rights, Boston, Mass. Dr Swiss directs the Women's Program, Physicians for Human Rights. Dr Giller formerly worked with the Medical Foundation of Kampala, Uganda.

Reprint requests to Women's Program, Physicians for Human Rights, 100 Boylston St, Suite 702, Boston, MA 02116 (Dr Swiss).

intended to disable an enemy by destroying the bonds of family and society. For example, the rape of women and girls in front of family members has been frequently reported during war.[10] The terrorism of rape sometimes forces entire communities into flight, further disintegrating community safeguards against rape.

In situations of ethnic conflict, rape can be both a military strategy and a nationalistic policy. As an expression of ethnic group hatred, rape of "enemy" women can be explicitly ordered or tacitly condoned by military authorities. In the former Yugoslavia, refugees described how public raping of women by military forces was used systematically to force families to flee their villages, achieving the goal of "ethnic cleansing."[12] In Burma, it has been reported that entire village populations fled into Bangladesh in cases of rape of "enemy" ladesh after Rohingya women were raped by the Burmese military.[13] A randomly chosen sample of 20 Ethiopian refugees who had fled forced relocation and ethnic persecution in Ethiopia were interviewed in a refugee camp in Somalia in 1986; 17 knew someone in their village, and 13 knew someone in their family, who had been raped by the Ethiopian militia.[14]

HUMAN RIGHTS ISSUES OF RAPE IN WAR

Treaties and other international agreements provide the legal basis for establishing prosecutions in cases of rape committed in wartime.[15-17] Evidence of rape by soldiers was first introduced in the Nuremberg War Crimes Trials, although it was not mentioned in any of the final judgments.[18,19] Rape was specifically identified as a war crime for the first time in the Tokyo War Crimes Trials after World War II, when commanders were held responsible for rapes committed by soldiers under their command.[20]

In January 1993, the UN sent a medical team to investigate rape in the former Yugoslavia. In light of evidence of rape perpetrated on a massive scale, the UN Commission on Human Rights passed a resolution placing rape, for the first time, clearly within the framework of war crimes and called for an international tribunal to prosecute these crimes.[21] In such a tribunal, individual soldiers and officers could be held accountable at several levels: those who committed rape, those who ordered it, and those in positions of authority who failed to prevent it.

The following sections examine some of the ways the medical community can support this process of accountability as well as perform its more usual role of treating individuals.

THE ROLE OF THE MEDICAL COMMUNITY

Documenting Incidents of Rape in War

Because the use of rape statistics for propaganda purposes is common during war, documenting rape—already difficult during peacetime—is even more challenging in the midst of war. While rape is known to be underreported in peacetime[22] (unpublished data, crime rate statistics on rape, Federal Agency of Statistics, Socialist Federal Republic of Yugoslavia, 1979 through 1988) because of the profound emotional pain and stigma attached to it, fear for the safety of family left behind and lack of ordinary support systems militate even further against disclosure during wartime. In a study of 107 Ugandan women who had been raped by soldiers, only half had told anyone about the rape incident as many as 7 years after the rape, despite the fact that all still had problems related to the rape when they finally spoke of it.[8]

Health care workers are in a unique position to recognize and document individual incidents of rape in war and to treat survivors. Women who have been raped often seek medical assistance, even when they fail to disclose the fact that they have been raped. It is important for health workers to be aware of common physical findings following rape, such as signs of violence to the genitalia (bruising, lacerations, or sometimes severe mutilation and damage to surrounding pelvic structures such as the bladder or rectum), bruising on the arms and chest,[8] and other evidence of the use of force such as patches of hair missing from the back of the head or bruising on the forehead (oral communication, Marian Chatfield-Taylor, MA, Connecticut Sexual Assault Crisis Services, February 1993). Because rape is often accompanied by beatings or other acts of torture, there may also be signs of violence to other parts of the body.[5,9,10,23,24] At the Cambodian refugee camp Site II in Thailand, special examination forms were created to document physical signs of sexual violence.[25]

Using Medical Data to Verify Widespread Rape

When the media first focused attention on the rapes in Bosnia, published estimates of the number of rape survivors fluctuated widely from 10 000 to 60 000. In most instances there appeared to be no method for arriving at the stated figures. While the true numbers may be very high, unsubstantiated claims risk creating questions about the credibility of the numbers themselves and the scale of

human rights violations against women in general.[26]

Using a public health approach, medical personnel can help provide evidence of the scale of these abuses. An illustration of this kind of documentation is provided by the international team of four physicians (which included one of us [S.S.]) sent by the UN to investigate reports of rape in the former Yugoslavia in January 1993. The medical team collected data on abortions, deliveries, known pregnancies due to rape, and sexually transmitted diseases. The team identified 119 pregnancies that resulted from rape from a small sample of six hospitals in Bosnia, Croatia, and Serbia.[11] According to estimates established in medical studies, a single act of unprotected intercourse will result in pregnancy between 1% and 4% of the time.[27,28] Based on the assumption that 1% of acts of unprotected intercourse result in pregnancy, the identification of 119 pregnancies, therefore, represents some 11 900 rapes. These numbers, however, must be interpreted carefully. Underreporting, along with the reluctance of many physicians to ask women seeking abortions or perinatal care whether they had been raped during the war, would lead to an underestimate of the number of women raped. On the other hand, multiple and repeated rapes of the same women were frequently reported and could lead to an overestimate of the number of women (as opposed to the number of incidents of rape) involved.[12] The goal is not to come up with an exact number, which is impossible, but rather to use medical data to suggest a scale of violations that cannot be determined from individual testimonies alone.

Using Techniques of Medical Science to Validate Testimony of Individual Rape

In most wars, soldiers are strangers to the women they rape, as both international and civil conflicts often take place between ethnic groups that were geographically separated before the war. In the case of the former Yugoslavia, however, dozens of testimonies have revealed that many women knew the names of, and often knew personally, the men who raped them.[12] While political events have led many to doubt whether war criminals will in fact be brought to justice in the former Yugoslavia, the UN Security Council has authorized the establishment of a war crimes tribunal. The following procedures, some of which are currently being used in criminal cases in the United States, could, in the future, help establish the identities of these perpetrators.

In countries at war, for women who

121

are able to seek gynecologic help within a day or two of being raped[29] (although most do not or are not able to), sperm collected from the genital tract could be dried on a microscope slide and stored for later analysis. For those women who become pregnant as a result of rape, placental tissue (following abortions or delivery) could be frozen and preserved for future testing. Alternatively, blood samples taken from the mother and child at any time could also be used. Matching of DNA or human lymphocyte antigen protein markers from such specimens can help determine paternity even many years later, using blood samples or hair follicles from the alleged perpetrator.[30] Medical services that are sufficiently organized to collect and safeguard the evidence would be able to help call alleged rapists to account.

Treatment of Individual Trauma

Medical services will frequently be the first recourse for women who have been raped because of injuries sustained or the fear of or actual symptoms of sexually transmitted diseases, including infection with the human immunodeficiency virus, or pregnancy.[4,6,8] It is important to address these medical needs by providing screening for sexually transmitted diseases, access to abortion, and obstetric and gynecologic services.

Having already suffered the trauma of rape, women who then become pregnant face further emotional and psychological trauma. Health care professionals in the former Yugoslavia have described responses of women including denial, severe depression, and neglect or rejection of the child after its birth.[12] While some women have been able to choose abortion, others, who lived in rural areas, were held captive, or lived in communities with religious prohibitions or laws limiting or denying access to abortion, may have had no choice but to bear an unwanted child.

Rape commonly results in severe and long-lasting psychological sequelae that are complex and shaped by the particular social and cultural context in which the rape occurs. Most of the data on the psychological effects of rape come from studies of adult Western women in peacetime who have suffered a single episode of rape. They describe both short-term and long-term effects. Commonly reported feelings at the time of the rape include shock, a fear of injury or death that can be paralyzing, and a sense of profound loss of control over one's life.[31-33] Longer-term effects can include persistent fears, avoidance of situations that trigger memories of the violation, profound feelings of shame,

difficulty remembering events, intrusive thoughts of the abuse, decreased ability to respond to life generally, and difficulty reestablishing intimate relationships.[11,34-36]

To understand the effects of rape in wartime, one must consider the additional trauma that women may have experienced: death of loved ones, loss of home and community, dislocation, untreated illness, and war-related injury. In addition, the common sequelae of rape described above may or may not be present in various cultural settings, and their relative importance may vary widely. It is critical to describe and address any psychological sequelae within the woman's cultural context. In any culture women may not voice their distress in "psychological" terms. For example, in the study of 107 Ugandan women raped during war,[8] only two presented with what could be termed psychological symptoms (nightmares and loss of libido). Fifty-three percent described their distress in physical complaints (headaches, chest pain, and rashes), and 57% in gynecologic symptoms, mainly vaginal discharge or pelvic pain, dating from the time of the rape. The persistence of perceived infection in this group, often despite multiple treatment for symptoms (approximately two thirds had no clinical findings of infection), reflects a common sequel to rape of feeling dirty and infected.[8] Similarly, Cambodian women who were raped during the Pol Pot period complained of vaginal discharge many years after the rape occurred.[27] Understanding the ways in which distress is expressed in particular cultural settings will shape responses to trauma. For Ugandan women, for example, it was important that their physical complaints were all treated as such. Once trust had been established between the health care workers and the women, it was then possible for the women to develop their own responses to rape trauma.

COMMENT

Certain tensions emerge in the roles of the medical community: (1) between the demand for adequate human rights documentation and the needs of the individual survivors of rape, (2) between the focus on individual healing and the emphasis on restoring bonds within the family and community, and (3) between the role of international medical assistance and the local medical community.

First, the very process of human rights documentation may conflict with the needs of individual survivors. Recounting the details of a traumatic experience may trigger an intense reliving of the event and, along with it, feelings of ex-

treme vulnerability, humiliation, and despair.[11] Health professionals in the former Yugoslavia have reported a number of harmful outcomes after survivors of rape have been interviewed by journalists, human rights workers, and even medical personnel. These include attempted or actual suicides, severe clinical depressions, and acute psychotic episodes.[12] Survivors require an environment that feels safe and contains adequate social support systems. They need to maintain control over when and where they talk about their experiences of abuse. Health care professionals can help ensure these safeguards by contributing to the development of guidelines that would limit further traumatization of rape survivors by assessing social and professional supports, ensuring voluntary consent and appropriate confidentiality, and structuring adequate collection of evidence.

Second, rape in war disrupts not only individuals but also social and community bonds (unpublished data, J.E.G., September 1992).[4,11,36,39] The restoration of these bonds, within a cultural framework that is free from the continuing effects of trauma, is fundamental to healing. For Ugandan women, the experience of rape disrupted their sense of community; keeping this aspect of their lives secret alienated them from other people. These women often expressed the fear that they would be rejected by their partners and the rest of the community.[8] The mending of social relationships was an important aspect of healing for them. Their response, once they felt that it was legitimate to talk about their experiences and to acknowledge that other women shared their own distress, was to organize themselves into meeting groups that focused on development projects and not specifically on their experiences of rape.[8]

In many cultures, interpersonal relationships rather than intrapsychic experiences are paramount, and the healing of social relationships will be an important starting point of therapy. This is at the center of much traditional healing. Community-based interventions that are sensitive to the local context and methods of healing may be the best approach to treating the wounds of rape in many situations. This is not to ignore or minimize the medical and psychological sequelae of rape, which may be severe, but rather to situate them in a cultural, social, and political framework that expands the therapeutic potential for overcoming the suffering engendered by rape.

Third, while the international medical community can share skills, for ex-

122

ample, in field-research techniques, which may enhance the community's resources and strengthen its responses to individual and community-wide trauma, its role must remain peripheral to that of the local community. Interventions are likely to succeed only if they do not create excessive dependence on imported expertise and solutions. Local personnel must be supported and encouraged in documenting rape, applying methods to aid accountability, and developing strategies for healing that are appropriate to the local community.

CONCLUSION

Health care professionals have a unique role to play in the investigation and documentation of rape in war as well as in the treatment of survivors. Collecting and presenting solid evidence will help hold perpetrators accountable, restore the rule of law, and limit future violations. Furthermore, increasing medical and social knowledge about rape in war will facilitate the development of strategies that foster the recovery of survivors of rape and their communities.

We thank Lori Heise; Anne Goldfeld, MD; Brinton Lykes, PhD; Paul Wise, MD; Herbert Spirer, PhD; Patrick Bracken, MA, MB, MRCPsych; Sarah Salter, JD; Tamara Tompkins; and the staff and board of directors of Physicians for Human Rights for their helpful comments and suggestions. Dr Swiss is grateful to Mary Anne Schwalbe and Susan Alberti of the Women's Commission for Refugee Women and Children for their support.

References

1. Brownmiller S. *Against Our Will: Men, Women, and Rape.* New York, NY: Simon and Schuster; 1975.
2. Sivard RL. *World Military and Social Expenditures 1991.* 14th ed. Washington, DC: World Priorities Inc; 1991.
3. Korean women drafted for sexual service by Japan: the comfort women issue. *Hearings Before the United Nations Secretary-General* (February 25, 1992) (testimony of Hyo-chai Lee, MA, Soon-Kum Park, and Chung-Ok Yun, MFA, Korean Council for the Women Drafted for Military Sexual Service by Japan).
4. Swiss S. *Liberia: Anguish in a Divided Land.* Boston, Mass: Physicians for Human Rights; 1992.
5. Swiss S. *Liberia: Women and Children Gravely Mistreated.* Boston, Mass: Physicians for Human Rights; 1991.
6. *Liberians: Our Forgotten Family: The Plight of Refugees and the Displaced.* New York, NY: The Women's Commission for Refugee Women and Children; 1991.
7. United Nations High Commissioner for Refugees. *Services for Vietnamese Refugees Who Have Suffered From Violence at Sea: An Evaluation of the Project in Thailand and Malaysia.* Geneva, Switzerland: United Nations High Commissioner for Refugees; February 1986:8.
8. Giller JE. *War, Women and Rape.* London, England: School of Oriental and African Studies, University of London; 1992. Thesis.
9. Giller JE, Bracken PJ, Kabaganda S. Uganda: war, women and rape. *Lancet.* 1991;337:604.
10. Goldfeld AE, Mollica RF, Pesavento BH, Farone SV. The physical and psychological sequelae of torture. *JAMA.* 1988;259:2725-2729.
11. Herman JL. *Trauma and Recovery.* New York, NY: HarperCollins; 1992.
12. *Report on the Situation of Human Rights in the Territory of the Former Yugoslavia.* Geneva, Switzerland: United Nations; 1993. United Nations document E/CN.4/1993/50.
13. *Burma: Rape, Forced Labor, and Religious Persecution in Northern Arakan.* Washington, DC: Asia Watch; 1992.
14. Clay J, Steingraber S, Niggli P. *The Spoils of Famine.* Cambridge, Mass: Cultural Survival Inc; 1988. Cultural Survival report 25.
15. The 1949 Geneva Conventions; the 1977 Protocols I and II; and the Convention Against Torture and Other Cruel, Inhuman or Degrading Treatment or Punishment. In: *Human Rights Documents.* Washington, DC: Committee on Foreign Affairs, US Congress; 1983.
16. The 1949 Geneva Conventions, Article 3. In: *Human Rights Documents.* Washington, DC: Committee on Foreign Affairs, US Congress; 1983.
17. The 1977 Protocol II to the Geneva Conventions. In: *Human Rights Documents.* Washington, DC: Committee on Foreign Affairs, US Congress; 1983.
18. *Trial of the Major War Crimes Tribunals Before the International Military Tribunal.* Nuremberg, Germany: Secretariat of the International Military Tribunal; 1947:6:393, 404-407.
19. *Trial of the Major War Crimes Tribunals Before the International Military Tribunal.* Nuremberg, Germany: Secretariat of the International Military Tribunal; 1947:7:456-457.
20. Pritchard RJ, Magbanua Zaide S, eds. *Tokyo War Crimes Trial.* New York, NY: Garland Publishing; 1981:20:49, 784-785, 791-792, 815-816, 820-821.
21. *Rape and Abuse of Women in the Territory of the Former Yugoslavia.* Geneva, Switzerland: United Nations; 1993. United Nations document E/CN.4/1993/L.21.
22. Hough M, Mayhew P. *British Crime Study.* London, England: Her Majesty's Stationery Office; 1983. Home Office Research Study 76.
23. Marcussen H, Rassmussen H, eds. *Examining Torture Survivors.* London, England: International Rehabilitation Council for Torture Victims and Amnesty International; 1991.
24. *Medical Testimony on Victims of Torture: A Physician's Guide to Political Asylum Cases.* Boston, Mass: Physicians for Human Rights; 1991.
25. Goldfeld AE. *End of Mission Report at Site II on the Thai-Cambodian Border.* Minneapolis, Minn: American Refugee Committee; July 1990.
26. Laber J. Bosnia: questions about rape. *N Y Rev Books.* March 25, 1993:3-6.
27. Cates W Jr, Blackmore CA. Sexual assault and sexually transmitted diseases. In: Holmes KK, Mardh P-A, Sparling PF, Wiesner PJ, eds. *Sexually Transmitted Diseases.* New York, NY: McGraw-Hill International Book Co; 1984:119-125.
28. Tietze C. Probability of pregnancy resulting from a single unprotected coitus. *Fertil Steril.* 1960;11:485-488.
29. *Rape in Kashmir: A Crime of War.* New York, NY: Physicians for Human Rights and Asia Watch; 1993.
30. King M-C. An application of DNA sequencing to a human rights problem. In: Friedman T, ed. *Molecular Genetic Medicine.* San Diego, Calif: Academic Press Inc; 1991;1:117-128.
31. Burgess AW, Holstrom LL. Rape trauma syndrome. *Am J Psychiatry.* 1974;131:981-986.
32. Santiago JM, McCall-Perez F, Gorcey M, Beigel A. Long-term psychological effects of rape in 35 rape victims. *Am J Psychiatry.* 1985;142:1338-1340.
33. Ellis EM, Atkeson BM, Calhoun AS. An assessment of long-term reactions to rape. *J Abnorm Psychol.* 1981;90:263-266.
34. Becker JV, Skinner LJ, Abel GG, Axelrod R, Cichon J. Sexual problems of sexual assault survivors. *Women Health.* 1984;9:5-19.
35. Becker JV, Skinner LJ, Abel BB, Treacy LC. Incidence and types of sexual dysfunctions in rape and incest victims. *J Sex Marital Ther.* 1982;8:65-74.
36. Ellis EM, Calhoun KS, Atkeson BM. Sexual dysfunction in victims of rape. *Women Health.* 1980;5: 39-47.
37. Pesavento BH. Treatment considerations for refugee children: learning from torture and abuse. Presented at the Harvard Medical School conference, Child Psychotherapy: Treating Children and Their Families in the '90s; June 18, 1993; Boston, Mass.
38. Bracken PJ, Giller JE, Kabaganda S. Helping victims of violence in Uganda. *Med War.* 1992;8:155-163.
39. Lykes MB, Brabeck MM, Ferns T, Radan A. Human rights and mental health among Latin American women in situations of state-sponsored violence: bibliographic resources. *Psychol Women Q.* In press.

123

Security Council

Distr.
GENERAL

S/1994/674
27 May 1994

ORIGINAL: ENGLISH

LETTER DATED 24 MAY 1994 FROM THE SECRETARY-GENERAL
TO THE PRESIDENT OF THE SECURITY COUNCIL

By its resolution 780 (1992) of 6 October 1992, the Security Council requested me to establish a Commission of Experts to examine and analyse information gathered with a view to providing the Secretary-General with its conclusions on the evidence of grave breaches of the Geneva Conventions and other violations of international humanitarian law committed in the territory of the former Yugoslavia. On 26 October 1992 I appointed a five-member Commission, chaired by Professor Frits Kalshoven and, following the latter's resignation, by Professor Cherif Bassiouni. My report on the establishment of the Commission of Experts was submitted to the Council on 14 October 1992 (S/24657).

The Commission commenced its activities in November 1992 and concluded its work in April 1994. During this period it has held 12 sessions and conducted a series of studies and on-site investigations, using for that purpose offers of assistance from Governments and non-governmental organizations. The Commission also established a database designed to provide a comprehensive record of all reported grave breaches of the Geneva Conventions and other violations of international humanitarian law. The two interim reports of the Commission, describing the status of its work and its preliminary conclusions were forwarded to the Security Council in my letters of 9 February 1993 (S/25274) and 5 October 1993 (S/26545).

The final report of the Commission includes a survey of the Commission's work since its inception, its mandate, structure and methods of work, its views on selected legal issues of particular significance in the context of the former Yugoslavia, a general study on the military structure of the "warring factions" and the strategies and tactics employed by them, and substantive findings on alleged crimes of "ethnic cleansing", genocide and other massive violations of elementary dictates of humanity, rape and sexual assault and destruction of cultural property committed in various parts of Bosnia and Herzegovina.

(d) The "President of the Republic", Mr. Hadzic, had approved the above-stated items and was willing to cooperate fully with the Commission.

276. Owing to weather conditions, the Commission had to postpone resumption of the investigation until the spring of 1994. In so far as the Commission's work was terminated as of 30 April, all relevant documents for this investigation have now been passed on to the Office of the Prosecutor for the International Tribunal. The site remains under UNPROFOR protection, but no criminal investigation related to this mass grave excavation has been conducted to date.

I. Investigation of grave sites near Pakračka Poljana (UNPA, Sector West, Croatia) 80/

277. During the March 1993 reconnaissance mission, the Commission became aware of the need to conduct a second mass grave excavation at a site, which would probably contain Serb bodies, at essentially the same time as the Ovčara excavation, which would probably be found to contain Croatian bodies. At the same time, it was informed of a number of probable clandestine grave sites near Pakračka Poljana in Sector West, which were believed to contain a large number of Serb bodies. For reasons related to the security of the sites and of potential witnesses, the Commission avoided visiting the sites at that time.

278. In October 1993, when the Commission was in a position to conduct a mass grave excavation, it decided to have Physicians for Human Rights conduct a preliminary site survey at Pakračka Poljana to confirm the existence of a mass grave. At the time this decision was taken, it was considered that the Pakračka Poljana location was the location in the United Nations protected areas (UNPAs) most likely to be the site of a mass grave containing Serb victims.

279. From 20 October to 9 November 1993, the Commission deployed teams to the area. The numbers of members of each group varied over time, as persons were shifted from the Ovčara site to Pakračka Poljana.

280. The Commission received a particularly high level of support from UNPROFOR during this investigation.

281. The forensic report on this preliminary site investigation reached the following conclusions:

(a) Nineteen individuals (16 males, 3 females) were buried in nine separate graves in a field south of Pakračka Poljana. The graves were shallow and appeared to have been dug by hand. Leaves found in the bottom of some graves and the clothing on several individuals, including heavy jackets and sweaters, suggests that burials took place in the autumn or early winter;

(b) The area around the graves was used as an execution site. Expended .22-calibre, .25-calibre, 9mm-calibre and 7.62 x 39mm-calibre cartridge cases were found adjacent to six of the graves. Expended rounds were also found near some of the bodies or recovered from clothing. Five of the bodies had their hands tied with rope. Other bodies had their hands together, sometimes in extremely awkward positions, but no rope was found during the excavations. It

/...

is possible that the hands had been bound but that the binding was made of a natural fibre that disintegrated. Fifteen of the bodies exhibited gunshot wounds to the head, two had blunt head trauma, one had multiple gunshot wounds to the arm and leg and one had massive head trauma;

(c) The nine graves are clandestine burials. The isolated location of the graves suggests that the executioners intended to bury their victims secretly. The graves were within a short distance of a road that could be accessed by a truck or other vehicle. The graves were also adjacent to large, woody vegetation that screened the area from at least one direction;

(d) There was no indication that the graves had been disturbed since the time of internment.

282. Although the Pakračka Poljana site was believed to be the site of mass graves containing up to 1,700 bodies, the site was examined with considerable care. Seventy-one holes were dug at the site. The very firmly based conclusion was reached that this belief was erroneous.

283. On 9 November 1993, the 19 exhumed bodies were placed in body bags together with preservative chemicals and reburied at a site immediately adjacent to an UNPROFOR observation post. Before this step was taken, some consideration was given to the possibility of conducting an autopsy examination of the bodies to establish identification and the cause/manner of death and to the possibility of gathering some additional ante-mortem information by interviewing selected persons in the area. These activities were not undertaken owing to previously expressed "Serb Republic of Krajina" concerns that post-mortems not be done in Croatia on account of the difficulty of obtaining a suitable morgue facility. Also, time and personnel resources would not permit the intensive effort required to conduct a criminal investigation and to gather all available ante-mortem information.

284. Responsibility for obtaining additional information and for continuing this investigation has now been passed to the Office of the Prosecutor of the International Tribunal.

J. Destruction of cultural property

285. In determining the extent of the destruction of cultural property in the former Yugoslavia, the Commission proceeded under its overall plan of work and made use more particularly of its database and reports by international organizations, including the United Nations Educational, Scientific and Cultural Organization (UNESCO), the Parliamentary Assembly of the Council of Europe and other intergovernmental sources and non-governmental organizations.

286. The Commission has received extensive information on destruction of cultural property, but it was not in a position to investigate all these allegations. In particular, it could not verify allegations that all Catholic churches and mosques in Serb-occupied territories of Bosnia had been systematically destroyed or damaged. Since the Commission could not consider,

/...

Appendix C

CITATIONS

[Roman letters in the citations equal enumeration of the documents in the table of authorities]

[Articles or other sources with a general character (in the sense of defining e.g. "killings" as human rights violations in general) are marked with (g), while the more specific ones are marked with (s)]

A. Abuses of rights guaranteed by medical neutrality

  1. *Infringements against medical personnel wounded and civilians*

    1.1 Killings or disappearances

        (a) Killings:
                        Arts. 4 para. 1, 27 I (g)
                        Art. 1 II (g)
                        Art. 3, j III (g)
                        Art. 55 c IV (g)
                        Arts. 1, 2, 15 para. 2 XII (g)
                        Arts. 2, 6 XV (g)
                        Arts. 2, 3 XXVIII (g)

                        Arts. 3 para.1, a, 12 VI (s)
                        Arts. 3 para.1, a, 12 VII (s)
                        Arts. 3 para.1, a, 13 VIII (s)
                        Arts. 3 para.1, a, 32 IX (s)
                        Arts. 10 para. 1, 75 para.2, a XX (s)
                        Arts. 4 para. 2, a, 7 para. 1 XXI (s)

        (b) Disappearances:
                        Art. 3, j III (g)
                        Art. 55 c IV (g)
                        Arts. 1, 2, 6, 7 XI (g)
                        Arts. 1, 2, 6, 7 XXII (g)
                        Arts. 2, 3 XXVIII (g)
                        Case, Section X, page 153 "crime against humanity"; Section XI, pp. 159-188 "State's duties"; XXX (g)

127

1.2 Torture or cruel, inhuman or degrading treatment

    (a) Torture:

                            Art. 5 paras. 1, 2, 3, Art. 27 I (g)
                            Art. 1 II (g)
                            Art. 3 j III (g)
                            Art. 55 c IV (g)
                            Arts. 1, 2 V (g)
                            Arts. 1, 2, 3, 4 X (g)
                            Arts. 1, 3, 15 para. 2 XII (g)
                            Arts. 1 - 8, 17 XIV (g)
                            Arts. 2, 7 XV (g)
                            Case, Part II, [1]-[4] XVIII (g)
                            Arts. 2, 5 XXVIII (g)

                            Arts. 3 para.1, a, 12 VI (s)
                            Arts. 3 para.1, a, 12 VII (s)
                            Arts. 3 para.1, a, 13 VIII (s)
                            Arts. 3 para.1, a, 32 IX (s)
                            Arts. 11 para. 2, 75 para. 2, a XX (s)
                            Art. 4 para. 2, a XXI (s)
                            Report XXIII (s)
                            Report XXIV (s)
                            Report XXV (s)
                            Report XXVI (s)

    (b) Inhuman or degrading treatment:

                            Art. 5 paras. 1, 2, 3 I (g)
                            Art. 25 II (g)
                            Art. 3, j III (g)
                            Art. 55 c IV (g)
                            Art. 1, 3, 15 para. 2 XII (g)
                            Art. 6 XIV (g)
                            Art. 2, 7 XV (g)
                            Case, Part II, [8] XVIII (g)
                            Arts. 3 para. 1, 12 VI (s)
                            Arts. 3 para. 1, 12 VII (s)
                            Arts. 3 para. 1, 13 VIII (s)
                            Arts. 3 para. 1, 32 IX (s)
                            Arts. 10 para. 2, 75 para. 1 XX (s)
                            Arts. 4 para. 1, 7 para. 2 XXI (s)
                            Case XVII (s)
                            Report XXIII (s)
                            Report XXIV (s)
                            Report XXV (s)
                            Report XXVI (s)

1.3 Serious harassment impeding medical funtions:

                Art. 3, j III (g)
                Art. 55 c IV (g)

                Art. 12 VI (s)
                Art. 12 VII (s)
                Art. 32 IX (s)
                Arts. 10 para. 2, 11 para. 4, 75
                para. 2, e XX (s)
                Arts. 4 para. 2, h XXI (s)
                Report XXIII (s)
                Report XXIV (s)
                Report XXV (s)
                Report XXVI (s)

1.4 Other:

                Art.12 XVI (g)=highest attainable
                standard of physical and mental
                health

2. *Infringements against medical facilities and services*

    2.1 Bombing or shelling of hospitals and clinics

        (a) Attacks upon medical personnel or units:

                Art. 3, j III (g)
                Art. 55 c IV (g)

                Arts. 19, 20, 35, 42 VI (s)
                Arts. 22 - 26 VII (s)
                Art. 33 VIII (s)
                Art. 20 IX (s)
                Art. 12 para.1 XX (s)
                Arts. 9 para. 1, 11 para.1 XXI (s)
                Report XXVII, page 13 (s)
                Report XXIX, page 21 (s)

        (b) Continuation of attacks:

                Art. 3, j III (g)
                Art. 55 c IV (g)

                Arts. 19, 21 VI (s)
                Arts. 22 - 26 VII (s)
                Art. 12 para. 3 XX (s)
                Arts. 9 para. 1, 11 para. 1˙XXI (s)
                Report XXVII, page 13 (s)

(c) Failure to provide sufficient warning:

        Art. 3, j III (g)
        Art. 55 c IV (g)

        Art. 21 VI (s)
        Art. 34 VII (s)
        Art. 13 para. 1 XX (s)
        Arts. 9 para. 1, 11 para. 2 XXI (s)
        Report XXVII, page 13 (s)

(d) Looting:

        Art. 3, j III (g)
        Art. 55 c IV (g)

        Arts. 19, 20 VI (s)
        Arts. 22 - 26 VII (s)
        Arts. 9 para. 1, 11 para. 1 XXI (s)

(e) Destruction or closure:

        Art. 3, j III (g)
        Art. 55 c IV (g)

        Arts. 19, 20, 35 VI (s)
        Arts. 22 - 26 VII (s)
        Arts. 9 para. 1, 11 para. 1 XXI (s)

(f) Knowing interruption of the supply:

        Art. 3, j III (g)
        Art. 55 c IV (g)

        Arts. 55 - 57 IX (s)
        Art. 14 XX (s)
        Report XXIX, page 21 (s)

2.2 Incursions into hospitals

(a) Arrest or detention:

        Art. 7 I (g)
        Arts. 1, 11, 25 II (g)
        Art. 3, j III (g)
        Art. 55 c IV (g)
        Arts. 2, 9 para. 1 XV (g)
        Arts. 2, 9 XXVIII (g)

                    Arts. 3 para. 2, 12 VI (s)
                    Arts. 3 para. 2, 12 VII (s)
                    Arts. 3 para. 2, 14, 30 VIII (s)
                    Arts. 3 para. 2, 16 IX (s)
                    Arts. 10, 11 XX (s)
                    Arts. 5, a, 7 para.1 XXI (s)

     (b) Expulsion or deportation; dismissal from job:

                    Art. 14 II (g)
                    Art. 3, j III (g)
                    Art. 55 c IV (g)

                    Art. 24 VI (s)
                    Arts. 32, 37 VII (s)
                    Art. 33 VIII (s)
                    Arts. 15 para. 1, 16 para. 1 XX (s)
                    Arts. 9 para. 1, 10 para. 1 XXI (s)
                    Report XXIX, page 21

2.3 Preventing the function of medical services in conflict
areas or occupied terretories:

                    Arts. 11, 14 II (g)
                    Art. 3 j III (g)
                    Art. 55 c IV (g)

                    Arts. 24, 35 VI (s)
                    Arts. 36, 37 VII (s)
                    Art. 33, a VIII (s)
                    Arts. 15 para. 4, 16 para. 2 XX (s)
                    Arts. 9 para. 1, 10 para. 2 XXI (s)

B. Abuse of responsibilities required by medical neutrality

   3. Abuse of medical facilities

     3.1 Use of hospital/clinic ambulance for military purposes:

                    Art. 3, j III (g)
                    Art. 55 c IV (g)

                    Art. 19 VI (s)
                    Arts. 12 para. 4, 15 paras. 2, 3 XX
                    (s)

                             131

Using medical personnel or units for military purposes:

        Art. 3, j III (g)
        Art. 55 c IV (g)

        Art. 19 VI (s)
        Art.   12   para.   4   XX   (s)

3.2 Abuse of medical emblem (red cross, red crescent):

        Art. 3, j III (g)
        Art. 55 c IV (g)

        Arts. 18, 44 VI (s)
        Art. 12 XXI (s)

4. *Abuse of medical skills*

4.1 Torture, cruel treatment, or military interrogation by medical personnel:

        Art. 55 c IV (g)
        Art. 1, 2 V (g)
        Art. 1, 2, 3, 4 X (g)
        Art. 1, 3, 15 para. 2 XII (g)
        Arts. 1 - 8 XIV (g)
        Art. 2, 7 XV (g)
        Art. 2, 5 XXVIII (g)

        Arts. 12, 18 para. 3 VI (s)
        Arts. 11 para. 4, 15 para. 3, 16 para. 2 XX (s)
        Arts. 9 para. 1, 10 para. 2 XXI (s)
        Report XXIII (s)
        Report XXIV (s)
        Report XXV (s)
        Report XXVI (s)
        Comment XIII, paras. 5, 7, 10 (s)
        Principles 1, 2, 4, 5, 6 XIX (s)

4.2 Selective and discriminatory treatment of wounded combatants or civilians on non-medical grounds:

        Art. 1 I (g)
        Art. 2 II (g)
        Art. 3, j III (g)
        Art. 55 c IV (g)

132

```
              Arts. 3 para. 1, 12 VI (s)
              Arts. 3 para. 1, 12, 30 VII (s)
              Arts. 3 para. 1, 16 VIII (s)
              Arts. 3 para. 1, 13, 27 IX (s)
              Comment XIII, paras. 5, 10 (s)
              Principles 1, 6 XIX (s)
              Arts. 10 para. 2, 15 para. 3, 75 XX
              (s)
              Arts. 2 para. 1, 7, 9 para. 2 XXI (s)
              Report XXIX, page 21
```

4.3 Medical treatment given according.to military instruction
rather than clinical indications:

```
              Art. 1 I (g)
              Art. 3, j III (g)
              Art. 55 c IV (g)

              Arts. 3 para. 1, 12 VI (s)
              Arts. 3 para. 1, 12, 30 VII (s)
              Arts. 10 para. 2, 15 para. 3 XX (s)
              Comment XIII, paras. 5, 7, 10 (s)
              Principles 1, 4, 5, 6 XIX (s)
```

4.4 Breach of medical confidentiality:

```
              Art. 3, j III (g)
              Art. 55 c IV (g)

              Art. 16 para. 3 XX (s)
              Art. 10 paras. 3, 4 XXI (s)
```

133

TABLE OF AUTHORITIES

I.   American Convention on Human Rights, November 22, 1969, OAS Treaty Series No. 36, OAS, OR, OEA/Ser. A/16 591.

II.   American Declaration of the Rights and Duties of Man, OAS, OR, OEA/Ser. L/V/E.23, Doc. 21, Rev. 2 (1948).

III. Charter of the Organization of American States, as amended by the Protocol of Buenos Aires of 1967, OAS Treaty Series No. 1-C, OAS, OR, OEA/Ser. A/2, Rev. (1970), 21 U.S.T. 607, T.I.A.S. 6847.

IV.   Charter of the United Nations, *signed* 26 June 1945, *entered into force* 24 October 1945, 59 Stat. 1031, T.S. No. 993, 3 Bevans 153.   Last amended 24 U.S.T. 2225, T.I.A.S. 7739.

V.   Convention Against Torture and Other Cruel, Inhuman or Degrading Treatment or Punishment (Annex), G.A. Res. 39/46, 10 December 1984, 39 U.N. GAOR Supp. (No. 51) 197, U.N. Doc. E/CN.4/1984/72.

VI.   Convention for the Amelioration of the Condition of the Wounded and Sick in Armed Forces in the Field (Geneva Convention I), 12 August 1949, 6 U.S.T. 3114, T.I.A.S. No. 3362, 75 U.N.T.S. 31.

VII. Convention for the Amelioration of the Condition of the Wounded, Sick and Shipwrecked Members of the Armed Forces at Sea (Geneva Convention II), 12 August 1949, 6 U.S.T. 3217, T.I.A.S. No. 3363, 75 U.N.T.S. 85.

VIII. Convention Relative to the Treatment of Prisoners of War (Geneva Convention III), 12 August 1949, 6 U.S.T. 3316, T.I.A.S. No. 3364, 75 U.N.T.S. 135.

IX.   Convention Relative to the Protection of Civilian Persons in Time of War (Geneva Convention IV), 12 August 1949, 6 U.S.T. 3516, T.I.A.S. No. 3365, 75 U.N.T.S. 287.

X.   Declaration on the Protection of All Persons from Being
        Subjected to Torture and Other Cruel, Inhuman or
        Degrading Treatment or Punishment, *adopted by* Fifth
        Congress on the Prevention of Crime and the Treatment of
        Offenders, Toronto, Canada, 8-12 September 1975, U.N.
        Pub. Sales No. 76.IV.2], G.A. Res. 3452 (XXX), 9 December
        1975, 30 U.N. GAOR Supp. (No. 34) 91, U.N. Doc. A/1034.

XI.   Declaration on the Protection of All Persons from
        Enforced Disappearance, G.A. Res. 47/133, 18 December
        1992, 47 U.N. GAOR Supp. (No. 49) 207, U.N. Doc.
        A/RES/47/133.

XII.   European Convention for the Protection of Human Rights
        and Fundamental Freedoms, *adopted* 4 November 1950,
        entered into force 3 September 1953, Euop., T.S. No. 5,
        213 U.N.T.S..

XIII.   General Comment No. 20 of the Human Rights Committee on
        the International Covenant on Civil and Political Rights,
        Report of the Human Rights Committee, *adopted* 3 April
        1992 by the Human Rights Committee, 47 U.N. GAOR, Supp.
        (No. 40), Annex VI a, U.N. Doc. A/47/40.

XIV.   Inter-American Convention to Prevent and Punish
        Torture, *adopted* 9 December 1985, *entered into force* 28
        February 1987, O.A.S. Treaty Ser. No. 67, O.A.S. Doc.
        OEA/Ser. P., AG/doc. 2023/85, Rev.1.

XV.   International Covenant on Civil and Political Rights,
        adopted 16 December 1966, *entered into force* 23 March
        1976, G.A. Res. 2200A (XXI), 21 U.N.
        GAOR Supp. (No. 16) 52, U.N. Doc. A/6316 (1967).

XVI.   International Covenant on Economic, Social and Cultural
        Rights, *adopted* 16 December 1966, *entered into force* 3
        January 1976, G.A. Res. 2200 (XXI), 21 U.N. GAOR, Supp.
        (No. 16) 49, U.N., U.N. Doc. A/6316 (1967).

XVII.   Ireland v. United Kingdom, 23 Eur. Ct. H.R. (Ser. B)
        (1976)

XVIII. *Filartiga v. Pena-Irala*, 630 F.2d 876, (2nd Cir. 1980).

XIX.   Principles of Medical Ethics Relevant to the Role of
        Health Personnel, Particularly Physicians, in the
        Protection of Prisoners and Detainees Against Torture and
        Other Cruel, Inhuman or Degrading Treatment or
        Punishment, G.A. Res. 37/194 (1982), 18 December 1982, 37
        U.N. GAOR Supp. (No. 51) 210, U.N. Doc. A/37/727.

XX.   Protocol Additional to the Geneva Conventions of 12 August 1949, and Relating to the Protection of Victims of International Armed Conflicts (Protocol I), *adopted* 8 June 1977, *entered into force* 7 December 1978, 1977 U.N. Jurid. Y.B. 95.

XXI.   Protocol Additional to the Geneva Conventions of 12 August 1949, and Relating to the Protection of Victims of Non-International Armed Conflicts (Protocol II), *adopted* 8 June 1977, *entered into force* 7 December 1978, 1977 U.N. Jurid. Y.B. 135.

XXII.   Question of Enforced or Involuntary Disappearances, Report of the Commission on Human Rights' Working Group on the Question of the Human Rights of All Persons Subjected to Any Form of Detention or Imprisonment, *presented* 31 January 1992 by the Human Rights Committee, U.N. Doc. E/CN.4/1991/19/Rev.1.

XXIII.   *Report of the Human Rights Committee*, U.N. GAOR, 44th Sess., Supp. (No. 40), Annex X, U.N. Doc. A/44/40, *Berterretche Acosta v. Uruguay*, Communication No. 162/1983, Views of the Human Rights Committee under article 5, paragraph 4, of the Optional Protocol to the International Covenant on Civil and Political Rights, *adopted* on 25 October 1988 at the thirty-fourth session.

XXIV.   *Report of the Human Rights Committee*, U.N. GAOR., 43rd Sess., Supp. (No. 40), Annex VII, U.N. Doc. A/43/40, *Cariboni v. Uruguay*, Communication No. 159/1983, Views of the Human Rights Committee under article 5, paragraph 4, of the Optinal Protocol to the International Covenant on Civil and Political Rights, *adopted* on 27 October 1987 at the thirty-first session.

XXV.   *Report of the Human Rights Committee*, U.N. GAOR., 43rd Sess., Supp. (No. 40), Annex VII, U.N. Doc. A/43/40, *Lafuente Peñarrieta et al. v. Bolivia*, Communication No. 176/1984, Views of the Human Rights Committee under article 5, paragraph 4 of the Optional Protocol to the International Covenant on Civil and Political Rights, adopted on 2 November 1987 at the thirty-first session.

XXVI.   *Report of the Human Rights Committee*, U.N. GAOR. 39th Sess., Supp. (No.40), Annex XI, U.N. Doc. A/39/40, *Viana Acosta v. Uruguay*, Communication No. 110/1981, Views of the Human Rights Committee under article 4, paragraph 4 of the Optional Protocol to the International Covenant on Civil and Political Rights, *adopted* on the twenty-first session.

XXVII.   *Report on the Situation of Human Rights in the Territory of the Former Yugoslavia*, Commission on Human Rights, 50th Sess., Agenda item 12, U.N. Doc. E/CN.4/1994/47.

XXVIII.   Universal Declaration of Human Rights', G.A. Res. 217A (III), 10 December 1948, 3 U.N. GAOR Supp. (No. 11A) 71, U.N. Doc. A/810, 7 (1948).

XXIX.   U.S.: Department of Defense Report to Congress on the Conduct of the Persian Gulf War - Appendix on the Role of the Law of War, 10 April 1992.

XXX.   *Velásquez Rodríguez*, Inter-American Court of Human Rights, Judgment of July 29, 1988, Series C No. 4 (case No. 7920(67)).

137

Security Council

Distr.
GENERAL

S/25274
10 February 1993

ORIGINAL: ENGLISH

LETTER DATED 9 FEBRUARY 1993 FROM THE SECRETARY-GENERAL
ADDRESSED TO THE PRESIDENT OF THE SECURITY COUNCIL

By resolution 780 (1992) the Security Council requested me to establish a
Commission of Experts with a view to providing me with its conclusions on the
evidence of grave breaches of the Geneva Conventions and other violations of
international humanitarian law committed in the territory of the former
Yugoslavia. The Commission commenced its work early in November 1992 and held
its third session in Geneva on 25 and 26 January 1993, following which it
transmitted to me a first interim report, together with a number of ancillary
documents, including a report of a preliminary site exploration of a mass
grave near Vukovar.

The interim report provides a broad view of the Commission's work to
date, its preliminary conclusions on the evidence examined and its views on a
number of important legal issues, and describes a plan of work for the next
stage of its activities.

I would particularly draw your attention to the following elements of the
interim report:

(a) Grave breaches and other violations of international humanitarian
law have been committed, including wilful killing, "ethnic cleansing" and mass
killings, torture, rape, pillage and destruction of civilian property,
destruction of cultural and religious property and arbitrary arrests;

(b) Because of the uneven value of much of the information provided,
verification of facts is essential;

(c) The Commission has identified and proposes to carry out on-site
investigations of alleged crimes in the Vukovar area, the mass grave near
Vukovar, detention camps and the allegations of systematic sexual assaults.

In respect of the proposed investigations, the Commission has indicated
that it intends to avail itself of offers of assistance from Governments and
non-governmental organizations. It has also requested that I establish a
trust fund to assist it in carrying out its mandate.

93-08351 4092b (E)   130293

[English only]

REPORT OF A PRELIMINARY SITE EXPLORATION
OF A MASS GRAVE
NEAR VUKOVAR, FORMER YUGOSLAVIA

19 January 1993

Physicians for Human Rights
100 Boylston Street
Suite 702
Boston, Massachussetts 02116
Tel. 617/695-0041
Fax. 617/695-0307

/...

CONTENTS

/...

140

REPORT OF A PRELIMINARY SITE EXPLORATION
OF A MASS GRAVE
NEAR VUKOVAR, FORMER YUGOSLAVIA

I. Executive Summary

On 17-19 December 1992, a 4-member international forensic
team, assembled by Physicians for Human Rights, conducted a
preliminary site exploration of a mass grave approximately 6 km
southeast of the city of Vukovar, in the territory of former
Yugoslavia. The work was carried out under the auspices of the
United Nations Commission of Experts, with escort and assistance
provided by the United Nations Protection Forces (UNPROFOR),
Sector East.

Based on the preliminary site exploration, the forensic team
concludes:

1. A mass execution took place at the gravesite.

2. The grave is a mass grave, containing perhaps as many
    as 200 bodies.

3. The remote location of the grave suggests that the
    executioners sought to bury their victims secretly.

4. There is no indication that the grave has been
    disturbed since the time of execution and interment.

5. The grave appears to be consistent with witness
    testimony that purports that the site is the place
    of execution and interment of the patients
    and medical staff members who disappeared during the
    evacuation of Vukovar Hospital on 20 November 1991.
    However, before that determination can be made with
    scientific certainty, the grave will need to be
    excavated and a number of bodies will need to be
    identified using forensic methods and procedures.

6. The fact that two bodies bore kneeklaces with
    Roman Catholic crosses--one bearing a small metal
    plate with the inscription "BOG I HRVATI" (God and
    Croatians)--suggests that the grave is likely to
    contain the remains of Croatians.

The forensic team proposes to return to Vukovar in mid-March
to continue its investigation of the site. This phase will
entail the complete excavation of the grave and the removal of
all of the bodies for medicolegal examination. To complete its
investigation, the forensic team will need the full support and
cooperation of the United Nations and interested governments as

/...

141

specified elsewhere in this report.

II. Introduction

On 17-19 December 1992, a 4-member international forensic
team, assembled by Physicians for Human Rights (PHR), conducted a
preliminary site exploration of a mass grave approximately 6 km
southeast of Vukovar, in the territory of former Yugoslavia. The
work was carried out under the auspices of the United Nations
Commission of Experts ("Commission"), which is charged under U.N.
security resolution 780 (1992) to collect and analyze evidence of
grave breaches of the Geneva Conventions and other violations of
international humanitarian law committed in the territory of the
former Yugoslavia. The members of the forensic team were Mr.
Eric Stover, PHR executive director; Dr. Clyde Collins Snow,
forensic anthropologist; Dr. Rebecca Ann Saunders, archeologist;
and Dr. Morris Tidball-Binz, medical doctor.

The grave was discovered by Dr. Snow and members of the
UNPROFOR Civilian Police (UNCIVPOL) in an isolated wooded area
southeast of the farming village of Ovcara, near Vukovar, on 18
October 1992. A preliminary inspection of the site revealed
three young adult male skeletons partially exposed by erosion and
animal scavengers. Two of the skeletons bore signs of perimortem
trauma (see Appendix A, Photo 1). Soon after the discovery of
the grave, UNPROFOR authorities took immediate action to insure
round-the-clock security of the site.

The discovery of the Ovcara site is consistent with witness
testimony of the disappearance of about 200 patients and medical
staff members from the Vukovar Hospital during the evacuation of
Croation patients from that facility on 20 November 1991.[1] At
that time, the hospital held several hundred civilian and
military patients, most of whom had been wounded in the heavy
fighting in and around Vukovar during the preceeding months.
When Serbian forces occupied the hospital in mid-November, both
sides agreed that the approximately 420 Croatian patients should
be evacuated to Croatian-held territory. According to this
agreement, the evacuation was to be monitored by representatives
of the European Monitoring Mission and the International
Committee of the Red Cross.

However, according to witnesses, reservists and Yugoslav
National Army (JNA) officers and soldiers separated the lightly

---

[1] See Annex II, U.N. Commission on Human Rights, "Report on the
situation of human rights in the territory of the former Yugoslavia
submitted by Mr. Tadeusz Mazowiecki, Special Rapporteur of the
Commission of Human Rights," E/CN.4/1992/S-1/10, 27 October 1992,
p. 13-14.

/...

wounded military and civilian males from the other patients and boarded them on several buses near the hospital. Among this group were a number of male hospital workers. The buses, each containing about 60 prisoners and two JNA guards, were driven to the JNA barracks in Vukovar at about 11:00. At 14:00 the buses proceeded to Ovcara where the men were transferred to a large building used as a garage for farm equipment and vehicles. While moving from the buses to the building, the men were beaten by JNA soldiers and Serbian paramilitaries with a variety of blunt instruments. The beatings continued for several hours inside the building. According to witness testimony, at least 2 men were beaten to death.

At about 18:00 that same day, JNA soldiers divided the prisoners into groups of about 20 men. One by one, each group was loaded onto a truck and driven away. At intervals of about 15 to 20 minutes, the truck returned empty and another group was loaded onto it. According to witness testimony, the truck left the building and turned onto a paved road that leads to Grabovo, a village about 3 km southeast of Ovcara. A few minutes later, the truck made a left turn onto a dirt field road. This road ran between a cultivated sunflower field on the left and a heavily wooded area on the right.

Given the estimates of time and distance between the farm building and from the description of the roads used, only one location fits the description: the dirt field road turning off the main road at 1.1 km southeast of the Ovcara complex. This track runs northeast, between a cultivated field on the left and a heavily wooded ravine on the right. The area where the skeletons were discovered is located at the head of the ravine, at 0.9 km from where the field road turns off the main road (see Appendix B, Map 1).

III. Field Report

The forensic team established five principal goals to be achieved during the on-site archeological survey. First, a detailed record and map of surface features of the site was to be completed. Second, a thorough surface survey of the site was to be conducted to determine if there was any evidence of a mass execution at or near the site. Third, a test trench was to be excavated through the site to establish the presence of a mass grave. Fourth, the site was to be examined so as to determine if it had been disturbed after the initial burial. Finally, preliminary forensic data were to be prepared for the skeletons exposed on the surface of the site.

/...

Surface Information

The site (hereafter referred to as OVC.1) lies at the northeast end of a ravine running northeast to southwest through cultivated fields (see Appendix B, Map 1). We arrived at the site around 10:30 on 17 December 1992. The perimeter of the site was secured with two rows of concertina wire. The UNPROFOR guard station, manned by Russian soliders, lay about 40 meters northeast of OVC.1; sentries were posted at intervals on the field road and in the fields surrounding OVC.1.

Before we conducted a surface survey of OVC.1, a UNPROFOR demining team checked the area for booby-traps and anti-personnel mines. The deminers found no such devices.

OVC.1 was located in a slough which contained large piles of fill dirt around the northern edge. This dirt contained garbage, including large animal bone (cow and pig), 5 gallon cans, veterinary supplies, and glass bottles, apparently derived from the farm. A dense secondary growth of burr bushes had volunteered in this fill. The gravesite, cut through these burr bushes and lacking vegetation except around the borders, was quite visible. Topographic features of the site included a large bulldozer pushup pile at the southeastern edge. This, and a clear blade impression running through the center of the grave, indicated that a bulldozer had been used to excavate and/or backfill the grave.

Our test trench, discussed below, demonstrated that the edges of the grave were defined by intermittent fracture lines in the earth, created as the grave settled and the more recently disturbed fill of the grave pulled away from the compacted fill dirt that served as the matrix (see Appendix B, Map 3). While the width of the grave was established in the area of the test trench (6.8 meters), the complete dimensions of the grave have not yet been determined. It may be significant that no bone was observed eroding out of the ditch in the southwest corner of the site.

Other surface features of the site included the remains of two individuals, referred to as Surface Skeleton 1 (SSK.1) and Surface Skeleton 2 (SSK.2). (A third individual, unnumbered and unexamined to date, is visible in a hole towards the northeastern edge of the grave.) As the appellations suggest, both these individuals had become fully skeletonized. The former was exposed on top of the pushup pile at the southeastern edge of the grave. When the site was first visited by Dr. Snow and UNCIVPOL personnel only the left humerus was visible. During their reconnaissance, additional elements of the skeleton were uncovered, including the cranium, left scapula, left ribs, and the left iliac crest, as well as some clothing. These remains were left undisturbed until we arrived at the site on 17

/...

144

December. Presumably this individual was caught up in the blade of the bulldozer during the final stages of backfilling. It is likely that no part of the body was visible a year ago, but that erosion of the soft dirt on top of the pushup pile subsequently exposed the humerus.

SSK.2 was located southeast of the site down a small footpath leading into the interior of the slough. Some longbones and additional clothing belonging to this individual were found spread out along the path. Rodent gnawing on some of these bones indicated that animals were possibly the agents of the dispersal of SSK.2. The main concentration of bones, including the cranium, ribs, and pelvis, was off to the left of the path some 17 meters from the edge of the gravesite proper.

The age of the vegetation in the area of SSK.2 indicated that there had been no filling and that the soils had not been disturbed within at least 5 years. Hence, another subsurface grave site attributable to the events at Vukovar is unlikely in this area.

SSK.1 and SSK.2 were removed from their locations and subjected to a preliminary forensic examination. These data are presented in Appendix C. Both of these individuals were males and the cause of death in both cases was gunshot wounds to the head. The skeletal remains and clothing of SSK.1 and SSK.2 were placed in large plastic bags by the forensic team. These bags were put at the extreme eastern end of the test trench and were covered with dirt as the test trench was backfilled.

Prior to any subsurface testing of the grave, a thorough surface survey was conducted in the area. Two kinds of evidence recovered during this survey indicated that an execution had occurred at the site. First, a large concentration of spent 7.62 mm cartridges of the type used in Kalishnikov firearms were found in the burr bushes northwest of the gravesite (see Appendix A, Photo 2). Some of these cartridges, as well as a "Serbian ammunition box," had been taken from the site by UNPROFOR personnel prior to our visit. However, well over 75 spent cartridges remained in the area. In contrast, no cartridges were present on the northeastern side of the grave or to the south. The locations of some cartridges were identified with pink flagging tape. Moreover, it is likely that a more thorough search, including inspection of the surface soil and grasses at this location, will reveal more spent cartridges.

The second, related, type of evidence consisted of numerous bullet scorings on the small acacia trees southeast of the site, including one tree just north of SSK.2 (see Appendix A, Photo 3). Bullets also penetrated a rusted vehicle chassis in the area.

/...

Subsurface Information

The presence of the two skeletons with gunshot trauma and the spent cartridges did not constitute sufficient evidence to indicate that the site was a mass grave. To confirm the interment of numerous individuals, we excavated a 1 meter by 7 meter test trench across the site. (The trench was later expanded 1 meter to the west in order to ensure that the western boundary of the grave was within the unit.) The test trench was established within a 7 meter by 9 meter unit that encompassed the major topographic features of the site. It should be noted, however, that the northern (or northwestern) edge of the gravesite, which could not be established on the basis of fracture lines, may lie 1 to 2 meters outside the unit. This distance is derived from the fact that spent cartridges were found on the surface at this distance from the northern edge of the unit.

Shovels were used to remove the fill within the test trench. When human remains were exposed in one portion of the trench, that area was pedestaled. Excavation ceased when human remains were exposed throughout the trench.

Because no individual was completely uncovered, and the individuals were buried with no consistent orientation, the exact number of individuals was impossible to determine. However, approximately nine individuals were exposed in the test trench (see Appendix B, Map 3). The shallowest interment was that of Test Trench Burial (TTB.3), which was located at just 22 centimeters below ground surface. The remainder of the burials were deeper, beginning around 60 centimeters below ground surface.

In contrast to the surface skeletons, the subsurface burials were quite well preserved. Clothing was more or less intact. Most tissue was present as adipocere; skin and hair were present. The deeper burials appeared bloated. While further excavation will prove unpleasant, the good preservation promises excellent recovery of both soft tissue and skeletal data.

A number of spent cartridges, one unspent projectile, and one tracer cartridge were recovered from the test trench during excavation. These were plotted and bagged. Three of the cartridges, including the tracer, were found below ground surface in the westernmost 1-meter of the trench, or outside the grave as presently defined. This may mean that these cartridges were present in the fill or that the western boundary of the grave may have to be revised. The bags containing all the cartridges were placed inside the larger bag containing the remains of SSK.2 and secured with that skeleton.

/...

146

Excavation inside the grave proper ceased at about 80 centimeters below ground surface. We did attempt to determine the total depth of the grave by digging a deeper test, or "sondage," within the trench at the extreme eastern edge of the grave. It was possible to follow the contour of the fill of the grave as it was distinct in color and texture from that of the surrounding fill matrix. Unfortunately, however, TTB.2 was against the wall of the grave and grave fill cut in sharply underneath that individual. Not wanting to undercut and destabilize this individual, we abandoned the sondage.

Before leaving the site, the team lined the floor of the trench with plastic sheeting and backfilled the trench.

Summary of Findings

Based on the preliminary site survey, the findings of the forensic team are as follows:

1. A bulldozer was used to cut through the secondary growth along the margins of the slough and to dig a grave within the pre-existing fill. The grave was approximately 9 X 7 meters. The exact boundaries of the grave, however, remain to be defined.

2. A mass execution took place at OVC.1. The executioners apparently lined up along the northern boundary of the grave, approximately 4 meters from the field road, and fired at their captives to the south and southeast. During the firing, spent cartridges were ejected to the right and many fell into the burr bushes on the southwest side of the grave. The bodies were then covered over by the bulldozer.

3. OVC.1 is a clandestine mass grave. The number of individuals within the relatively small "window" of the test trench, as well as the disposition of the bodies, indicate that a mass grave is present and that it may contain as many as 200 bodies. The remote location of the grave suggests that the executioners intended to bury their victims secretly. Moreover, it appears that SSK.2 may have been attempting to flee the scene, but was shot and left lying in the wooded area behind the grave.

4. There is no indication that OVC.1 has been disturbed since the time of execution and interment.

5. OVC.1 appears to be consistent with witness testimony that purports that the site is the place of execution and interment of the patients from Vukovar Hospital. However, before that determination can be made with scientific certainty, OVC.1 will need to be excavated and a number of bodies will need to be identified using forensic methods and procedures.

/...

147

6. Finally, the fact that two bodies bore knecklaces with Roman Catholic crosses--one bearing a small metal plate with the inscription "BOG I HRVATI" (God and Croatians)--suggests that the grave is likely to contain the remains of Croatians (see Appendix A, Photo 4).

IV. Antemortem Information

In Zagreb, the forensic team met with doctors who are members of the Joint Commission to Trace Missing Persons and Mortal Remains. This commission, which is comprised of Croatian and Serbian doctors and forensic specialists, meets periodically in Budapest to exchange information about persons believed to have been killed or are missing as a result of the war. We received from the commission a list of the names, and some antemortem information, of those patients and medical personnel from the Vukovar Hospital who are still missing (see Appendix D). The commission will continue to gather antemortem data.

The forensic team gave members of the commission photographs of the necklaces found on SSK.1 and SSK.2, as well as a photograph the small figurine of a saint found wrapped in cloth on SSK.2. These photographs should be distributed to relatives of the missing from Vukovar Hospital.

V. Recommendations: Excavation & Medicolegal Investigation

The forensic team is now ready to begin the second phase of the investigation of OCV.1. This phase will entail the complete excavation of the grave and the removal of all of the bodies for laboratory analysis. At present, the forensic team plans to return to Vukovar in mid-March to continue the excavation of Ocv.1. The excavation phase will take 3-4 weeks; the medicolegal examination phase will take 4-6 weeks.

To complete the investigation of the Ovcara grave, the forensic team will require the full support and cooperation of the U.N. Secretary General, the U.N. Security Council, the U.N. Commission of Experts, UNPROFOR, and interested governments which may be called on to provide logistical support. The forensic team will require the following commitments and logistical support:

1. The U.N. Commission of Experts should appoint one of its members to act as a direct liaison with the forensic team.

2. The U.N. Secretary General and/or the U.N. Security Council should instruct all U.N. agencies to cooperate and provide logistical support to the forensic team during the course of the investigation of OVC.1 and other mass grave sites. They

/...

148

should also call on governments to assist the forensic team by
providing it with the various logistical supplies specified
below.

3. The U.N., at the highest level, should issue a written
statement to the effect that the Ovcara grave is under U.N.
jurisdiction. The U.N. should authorize the Commission of
Experts, through its forensic team, to remove the bodies and
other artefacts from the grave so that they may be examined in a
secure place. The U.N. should also instruct UNPROFOR to provide
additional protection for the site during the course of the
excavation. This procedure should be followed in all subsequent
investigations of individual or mass graves associated with
apparent war crimes in the territory of former Yugoslavia.

4. On-site Excavation: The forensic team will need the
following supplies in order to carry out the excavation of the
grave in a quick and efficient manner:

o Four (4) container units, similar to the ones now
being supplied to UNPROFOR by the Finnish
government. Two (2) of the containers should be
a refrigeration unit, which should be used to
store the bodies either on the site or at
the Vukovar Barracks. An alternative would
be several "temp tents," similar to those used
by the United States military.

o Two (2) water pumps and a generator to drain
water from the site.

5. Vukovar Barracks: For security reasons, the forensic
team should be housed in the Vukovar Barracks (UNPROFOR) for the
duration of the excavation. This will require:

o Five (5) housing units and 1 shower/disinfecting unit
similar to the ones supplied to UNPROFOR by the
Finnish government.

6. Transportation of the Bodies: To maintain security and
chain-of-custody of the bodies and other artefacts from the site,
UNPROFOR should be in charge of transporting them from the grave
to the Vukovar Barracks and then, by air or overland, to UNPROFOR
headquarters at the Zagreb airport.

7. Medicolegal Examination: The medicolegal examination of
the bodies and artefacts will be conducted by an international
team of forensic specialists in pathology, radiology, physical
anthropology, and odontology. The team will need a facility that
has hot and cold running water, adequate space and lighting,
ventilation and heating, X-ray capabilities, basic autopsy
tables, and refrigeration units for storage of the bodies. If

/...

149

the facility is located in Zagreb, it will need to be kept under
UNPROFOR jurisdiction to maintain security and chain-of-custody.
Our first choice would be to conduct the medicolegal examination
of the bodies in the area where the 212 U.S. Mash Unit is now
operating at the Zagreb airport. However, X-ray units would need
to be brought in. An alternative would be to transport the
bodies to an vacant hangar or warehouse near a military air base
(or possibly a civilian airport) somewhere in Europe. The
international forensic team could examine the bodies at this
facility, so long as it was equipped with the items listed above.

After the forensic team completes its medicolegal
examination, the bodies should be handed over to the Joint
Commission to Trace Missing Persons and Mortal Remains, based at
the University of Zagreb Medical School.

/...

MAP 2 -- OVC.1 Site Map

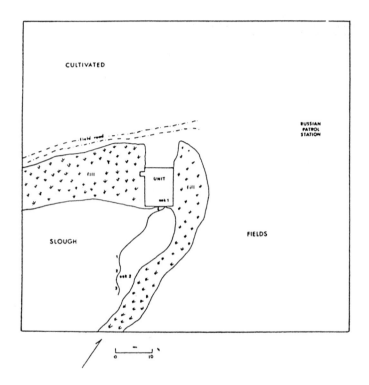

151

/...

Map 2.   OVC.1 Site Map.

Key:

1.   Left tibia and fibula of SSK 2.
2.   Right tibia and fibula of SSK 2.
3.   Human ribs and sweatshirt probably belonging to SSK 2.
4.   Vehicle chassis with bullet holes.

MAP 3 -- OVC.1 Unit with Test Trench

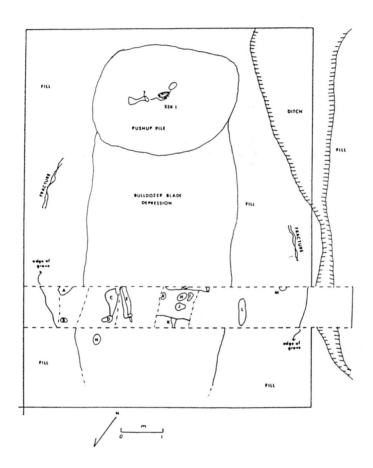

Map 3.   OVC.1 Unit with Test Trench.

Key:

A. Soft tissue, depth .68 meters below ground surface (mbgs).
B. Clothing, Test Trench Burial 2, depth .72 mbgs.
C. Possible pants leg, depth .57 mbgs.
D. Boot or shoe, depth .48 mbgs.
E. Shirt, with hand exposed, Test Trench Burial 3,
    depth .22 mbgs.
F. Clothing, depth .64 mbgs.
G. Pants leg with sock, Test Trench Burial 4, depth .44 mbgs.
H. Skin, depth .50 mbgs.
I. Clothing, depth .50 mbgs.
J. Cranium, Test Trench Burial 5, depth .58 mbgs.
K. Sweater, belt, pants, Test Trench Burial 6, depth .74
    mbgs.
L. Clothing, Test Trench Burial 7, depth .37 mbgs.
M. Sock, Test Trench Burial 8, depth .51 mbgs.

Note: No Test Trench Burial 1 number was assigned. Numbers given
are those burials photographed individually. Estimated number of
individuals exposed within the trench is nine.

APPENDIX C

PRELIMINARY DESCRIPTIONS OF TWO SKELETONS FOUND ON SURFACE

AT OVCARA SITE ONE

Both of these skeletons were found on the surface at the
Ovcara site. They were examined in the field under less than
optimum conditions so that the results presented here should be
considered preliminary until a more complete and adequate examination can be made under laboratory conditions. After examination, the each skeleton, along with its associated clothing was
placed in a labelled plastic bag and buried in the exploratory
test trench in order to secure them until they can be recovered
for a more detailed examination.

SURFACE SKELETON #1 (SSk1)

This skeleton was first observed during the initial examination of the site on October 18, 1992. It was located in the area
of pushed-up earth at the southeastern section of the site.
Initially, only the left humerus was exposed. Some of the earth
was cleared from around the skull and left shoulder skeleton. A
gunshot wound of exit was observed in the left temple.

Since at that time UNPROFOR officials were concerned that
the site might be disturbed or even destroyed by locals before it
could be properly secured, the left scapula was photographed in
situ, labelled and removed in order to serve as evidence that
human remains were indeed present at the scene when it was first
examined. The remaining bones were left undisturbed. The
scapula remained in custody of SECTOR EAST CIVPOL authorities
until we returned in December to more fully explore the site. At
that time, it was returned to the site and reburied with the
other SSK1 remains in the test trench.

Determination of Sex

The skeleton is diagnosed as male on the basis of pelvic
morphology. The innominate bones display the typical masculine
features of a highly-arched iliac crest, acute sciatic notch,
everted ischiopubic ramus and the subtriangular pubes. Cranial
morphological features are also strongly male and include large
supraorbital brow ridges, robust mastoid processes and strongly
developed nuchal musculature margins.

Age at Death

Long bone epiphyses, including the medial clavicular, are
fully closed, although the latter displays signs of fairly recent
union. The first and second sacral segments are unfused. These
findings are consistent with an age of around 23 to 31 years.
This range can be narrowed somewhat based on pubic symphsial

/...

155

morphology. Using the McKern-Stewart standards the pubic symphy-
sis is scored at 4, 2.5, 1 corresponding to a pubic age of about
23 ± 2 years. Therefore, a final age estimate of around 25 ± 3
years appears reasonable.

Diagnosis of Race

Cranial morphological features are strongly Caucasoid.
These include the mesocranic vault, long face, relatively narrow
nasal aperture and high nasal bridge.

Antemortem Stature

Using the Trotter-Glesser regression equations for calculat-
ing antemortem stature of Caucasoid males from the combined
lengths of the femur (476 mm) and tibia (405 mm), antemortems
stature is estimated at 178 cm with a SEest of 3.00 cm. This
yields a .95 probability range of 172 to 184 cm.

Handedness

Scapular beveling, long bone musculature attachments are
more strongly developed on the right. The right forearm bones
exceed the left in length by several millimeters. These features
indicate that the decedent was right-handed.

Individuation

The skeleton displayed no apparent signs of anomalies or
antemortem pathologies which might be reflected in the decedent's
medical history. However, since this examination was conducted
under field condtions, the presence of such features should not
be entirely ruled out until a more detailed laboratory examination of the flesh-free bones can be made.

Dentally, the strong labial displacement of the right maxil-
lary canine would be a feature recognised by the family and
friends of the decedent. It might also be apparent in any
photographs of the decedent shown smiling.

Dental Observations

Pending a detailed examination and charting of the dentition
under laboratory conditions, only the salient dental findings
will be noted. These were as follows:

Tooth No. (Universal)	Condition
1.	Not present
4.	Occluso-distal amalgam filling
6.	Buccal displacement by #7
7.	Strong lingual displacement
10.	Missing antemortem
16.	Not present
18.	Missing antemortem
19.	Missing antemortem
20.	Small gold foil filling?
30.	Massive caries, alveolar abcess
31.	Massive caries

156

Clothing
        The following clothing items were found with the remains:
            1. Loose-knit black sweater
            2. Black or dark-blue T-shirt bearing "LINATTENOY"
            3. Red long underwear
            4. Levi-Straus blue jeans, made in Yugoslavia
            5. Heavy leather belt with iron buckle
            6. Red socks

In addition to the above items, a leather shoe was found near the
remains but was not directly associated with them.

Personal Effects
        These consisted of three items suspended from a   chain
found around the decedent's neck: 1. metal cross, 2. small gold
clover leaf, 3. a silver-colored medallion bearing the inscription "BOG I HVARTI"

Time of Death
        This estimate is based on the general condition of the
remains which were partially disarticulated, but retaining
consideralble amounts of soft tissue in an advanced state of
decomposition. The cranial cavity still contained a large mass
of semi-liqufied cerebral tissue. Considering the fact that the
remains were still partially earth-covered when first examined a
time of death of 6-18 months prior to discovery seems reasonable.

Cause of Death
        A single, small caliber gunshot entrance wound is located in
the right parietal, 1 cm posterior to the coronal suture and 4 cm
right of the saggital suture. Two irregularly-shaped, externally-beveled exit wounds are present on the left cranial vault.
The anteriormost is in the left pterionic region; the posterior
wound is in the left temporal squama immediately posterior to the
transverse temportal crest. Additionally, there is a large
defect in the petrous portion of the temporal bones.
        The observed trauma is consistent with a single bullet
entering the right parietal and passing transversely, inferiorly
and slightly posteriorly to exit as three fragments in the left
pterio-temporal region

SUMMARY OF FINDINGS: SSk1
        This skeleton is that of a adult caucasoid male who was
between 23 and 28 years old at the time of death which occurred
about 6-18 months prior to the first examination of the body in
December, 1992. He was around 178 ± 6 cm tall and right-handed.
The cause of death was a gunshot wound of the head, with the
bullet entering the right side of the cranial vault with downward
and backward transverse trajectory.

157

SURFACE SKELETON #2 (SSk2)

This skeleton was first observed on the intial visit to the Ovcara site on October 18, 1992. It was lying in the southeast of the mass grave burial in an area wooded by small acacia saplings, along a path leading away from the burial site. The main concentration, including the skull, pelvis and most of the trunk and extremity bones lay immediately to the left of the path. This area apparently marked the original location of the body. Several extremity bones, some ribs, as well as some of the clothing were found several meters from the main concentration - apparently they had been drug away by small animal scavengers. at some stage of post-mortem decomposition. Many of the bones showed damage caused by gnawing by small rodents. At the time of intial discovery, the bones were left in situ. Upon our return in December, the site was found undisturbed except for the cranium which had been moved approximately one meter from its original location. This may have been done by an medical officer of the UNPROFOR BritMed Unit who later reported that he made an inspection of the site on October 19, before it had been fully secured by RUSSBAT troops.

Determination of Sex
Sex was determined to be male on the basis on pelvic morphology which displayed the typical masculine features of a highly-arched iliac crest, narrow subpubic and sciatic angles, everted ischio-pubic rami and subtriangular pubes. Cranial features were also robustly male and included large mastoids, heavy surpraorbital brow ridges and strongly developed nuchal musculature attachements.

Estimation of Age
Long bone epiphyses, including the medical clavicular were fully closed as were the sacral S1-2 segments. These findings are consistent with an age of at least 24 years at the time of death. Pubic symphsial morphology also suggested an age in the mid-20s. A final age estimate of 24 to 32 years appears reasonable.

Diagnosis of Race
Cranial racial indicators are strongly Caucasoid. These include the mesocranic cranial vault, relatively long facial skeleton, narrow nasal aperture, and salient nasal bridge and orthognathous facial profile.

Antemortem Stature
As noted above, small animals had damaged most of the long bones of the extremities, leaving only the left radius intact. This measured 255 mm. Using the Trotter-Glesser equations for predicting antemortem stature from the radius in caucasoid males, an estimate of 175.5 cm ± 4.3 SEest. is derived. From this, a .95 probability range for stature is 167 to 184 cm.

158

Handedness
Scapular beveling was pronounced on the right. The right forearms displayed heavier muscle attachments and were slightly longer than the left. These findings indicate that the decedent was right-handed.

Individuation
No skeletal evidence of old anomalies, injuries or diseases which would be reflected in the decedent's medical history were observed. However, since the examination was made in the field, such findings may be discovered when a fuller examination of the cleaned bones can be made under laboratory conditions.

Dental Observations
The dentition displays a number of features which would be undoubtedly reflected in his dental records should these be obtained. Until a fuller examination can be made under laboratory conditions, the following observations should be considered provisional.

TOOTH NO. (Universal)	OBSERVATION
2.	Occlusal amalgam
3.	Mesio-occlusal & disto-lingal amg.
13. - 16.	Missing antemortem
18.	Occluso-buccal amg.
19.	Mesio-occluo-distal amg.
20.	Occlusal amg.
22.	Lingually displaced
28.	Mesio-occlusal amg.
29.	Occlusal amg.
30.	Mesio-occlusal-distal amg.
31.	Mesio-occlusal-buccal amg.

Clothing
Clothing found with the victim consisted of a dark blue sweatshirt. On the front is the legend "QUEBEC CANADIAN PACIFIC" below which appears "Candian Pacific". On the back there is a winter scene with a skier in the foreground, ice skaters in the background. To the right of the skier are the words "Winter Sport" and below that "Candian Pacific".

Personal Effects
A gold chain with two crosses and a small gold horseshoe inset with a ladybug. Also found was a small clear plastic pouch containing a small gold-colored statuette of a male saint holding a child.

159

Time of Death

The skeleton was completely disarticulated with the exception of the pelvic elements and some of the vertebral segments. Other soft tissue remnents were limited to tags of dried ligaments and hair. Based on the condition of the bones, and the exposure environment, time of death is estimated at about 6-18 months prior to examination of the skeleton in December, 1992.

Cause of Death

Perimortem trauma consisted of almost complete destruction of the midfacial area. The fracture pattern is consistent with a wounds caused by high-velocity gunshot. However, until the remains can be more fully examined under laboratory conditions, the diagnosis of fatal gunshot injury must be considered provisional.

SUMMARY OF FINDINGS: SSk2

The skeleton is that of a caucasoid male who was somewhere between 24 and 32 years of age at the time of his death which occurred about 6-18 months prior to examination. He was around 176.5 cm tall (167-184 cm .95 p range) and right-handed. Perimortem destruction of the midfacial skeleton is consistent with a high-velocity gunshot wound to the head.

160

Appendix E

D 5/216 BIS - D 1/216 BIS   3/216 BIS   qucf,

<u>INTERNATIONAL CRIMINAL TRIBUNAL</u>
<u>FOR THE FORMER YUGOSLAVIA</u>

<u>Case no. IT-95-13-I</u>

Before: JUDGE FOUAD RIAD

Registrar: MRS. DOROTHÉE DE SAMPAYO GARRIDO-NIJGH

Decision of 7 November 1995

THE PROSECUTOR

v.

MILE MRKŠIĆ
MIROSLAV RADIĆ
VESELIN ŠLJIVANČANIN

CONFIRMATION OF THE INDICTMENT

<u>The Prosecutor</u>
represented by:

Mr. Graham Blewitt
Mr. Clint Williamson

161

INTERNATIONAL CRIMINAL TRIBUNAL
FOR THE FORMER YUGOSLAVIA

THE PROSECUTOR OF
THE TRIBUNAL

AGAINST

MILE MRKŠIĆ
MIROSLAV RADIĆ
VESELIN ŠLJIVANČANIN

INDICTMENT

Richard J. Goldstone, Prosecutor of the International Criminal Tribunal for the
Former Yugoslavia, pursuant to his authority under Article 18 of the Statute of the
International Criminal Tribunal for the Former Yugoslavia (Tribunal Statute), alleges:

1.   This indictment charges persons responsible for the mass killing at Ovčara,
near Vukovar, Croatia, of approximately 260 captive non-Serb men who had been
removed from Vukovar Hospital on 20 November 1991.

2.   The city of Vukovar is located in the Eastern Slavonian region of Croatia on
the banks of the Danube River, which there marks the border between the Republic of
Serbia and the Republic of Croatia. In the 1991 census, the population of the Vukovar
municipality, which included the city and surrounding villages, was 84,189 of which
36,910 were Croat (43.8 %), 31,445 Serb (37.4 %), 1,375 Hungarian (1.6 %), 6,124
Yugoslav (7.3 %), and 8,335 others (9.9 %).

3.   After a 19 May 1991 referendum in the Republic of Croatia regarding
Croatia's future in the Yugoslav federation, Croatia declared its independence on 25
June 1991. At the urging of the European Community, the effective date of
independence was postponed until 8 October 1991.

4.   Soon after the 25 June 1991 declaration of independence, Serbs living in
Croatia intensified the armed insurrection they had begun several months earlier,
which the Croatian authorities attempted to suppress. The federal Yugoslav Peoples
Army (JNA) intervened in support of the Serb insurgents.

5.   After attacking some of the surrounding villages that were inhabited mostly by
non-Serbs, by late August 1991, the JNA had surrounded the city of Vukovar and was
laying siege to it. In conjunction with the siege, the JNA engaged in a sustained
artillery assault on the city, killing hundreds of persons and destroying most of the
buildings in the city. The JNA and Serb paramilitary forces also launched infantry
and armoured attacks that ultimately led to the fall of Vukovar on 18 November 1991.
The JNA and Serb paramilitary forces then occupied what remained of the city.

162

6.   The JNA unit with primary responsibility for the attack and subsequent occupation of Vukovar was the Belgrade-based Guards Brigade, commanded by Colonel Mile MRKŠIĆ. Subordinate to Colonel MRKŠIĆ was Major Veselin ŠLJIVANČANIN, who had direct operational command of JNA forces in the immediate area of the city. Major ŠLJIVANČANIN was the security officer for the Guards Brigade, and he also commanded a military police battalion which was part of the brigade. Another part of the brigade that took an active role in the siege and occupation of the city was the special infantry unit commanded by Captain Miroslav RADIĆ, a close associate of Major ŠLJIVANČANIN.

7.   In the last days of the siege, several hundred people sought refuge at Vukovar Hospital, which was near the city centre, in the belief that it would be evacuated in the presence of neutral international observers. This evacuation had been agreed upon in Zagreb in negotiations between the JNA and the Croatian government on 18 November 1991. In addition to the sick and wounded, civilians, families of hospital staff, and soldiers who had been defending the city, some posing as patients or hospital staff, gathered on the hospital grounds.

8.   On the afternoon of 19 November 1991, JNA units arrived at Vukovar Hospital and took control of it. Those inside offered no resistance. Early the following morning, Major ŠLJIVANČANIN ordered the nurses and doctors to assemble for a meeting. While the medical staff was attending this meeting, JNA and Serb paramilitary soldiers hurriedly removed about 400 men from the hospital. Among those removed in this way were wounded patients, hospital staff, soldiers who had been defending the city, Croatian political activists, and other civilians. By the time the medical staff meeting with Major ŠLJIVANČANIN concluded, the soldiers had removed almost all of the men who were at the hospital.

9.   The soldiers loaded about 300 of these men onto buses and held them on the buses under JNA guard. Later that morning, the buses left the hospital compound and proceeded through the centre of Vukovar to the JNA barracks on the south side of the city. The men were kept inside the buses at the barracks for about two hours. During that time, on orders from Major ŠLJIVANČANIN, about 15 of the men were removed from the buses, apparently because the men were part of the hospital staff or were related to staff members.

10.   The remaining men were then driven to a building at the Ovčara farm, about four kilometres southeast of Vukovar. There JNA and Serb paramilitary soldiers took the men from the buses and forced them to run between two lines of soldiers, who beat the men as they passed. Inside the farm building, the soldiers continued to beat the men for several hours. At least two men died from the beatings. About seven of the men were released after Serbs who were present intervened on their behalf. These men were driven back to Vukovar.

11.   The remaining men were held in the building at Ovčara. The Serb authorities listed identifying information about each man and then divided the men into groups of ten to twenty. The soldiers loaded each group in turn into a truck which left the farm building with the group and then returned empty a short while later.

12.   The truck travelled south from the Ovčara farm building on the road leading to Grabovo. Approximately one and one-tenth kilometres southeast of the building, the

163

truck turned left and then travelled northeast on a dirt field road which ran between a cultivated field on the left and a wooded ravine on the right. At the head of the ravine, approximately 900 metres from the Ovčara-Grabovo road, the soldiers removed the men from the truck.

13.   At this spot, JNA and Serb paramilitary troops under the command and supervision of Colonel Mile MRKŠIĆ, Captain Miroslav RADIĆ and Major Veselin ŠLJIVANČANIN were assembled on the north side of the site. During the evening hours of 20 November 1991, these soldiers, firing in a southerly direction, shot and killed about 260 men. After the killings, the bodies of the victims were buried by a bulldozer in a mass grave at the same location.

14.   Of the 300 men taken from Vukovar Hospital on the morning of 20 November 1991, 261 remain missing. All of these men were alive after the end of hostilities in Vukovar, and all of these men were taken under JNA guard first to the JNA barracks and then to the Ovčara farm. They have not been seen alive since that time. The names of these men, with their fathers' names in parenthesis, and their dates of birth are as follows:

Adžaga, Jozo (Ilija)	21.05.49
Andrijanić, Vinko (Marko)	09.02.53
Anić-Antić, Jadranko (Ante)	19.04.59
Arnold, Krešimir (Alojz)	18.04.58
Asadanin, Ilija (Jovan)	01.01.50
Babić, Dražen (Josip)	01.10.66
Bainrauch, Ivan (Stjepan)	21.06.56
Bajnrauh, Tomislav (Franjo)	13.12.38
Baketa, Goran (Stojan)	28.06.60
Balaš, Stjepan (Andrija)	01.05.56
Balaž, Vesna (Jozo)	06.09.55
Balog, Dragutin (Josip)	19.06.74
Balog, Josip (Dragutin)	25.11.28
Balog, Zvonko (Ivan)	10.01.58
Balvanac, Đuro (Andrija)	17.07.52
Banožić, Boris (Drago)	02.02.67
Baranjaji, Pero (Ratko)	19.06.68
Barbarić, Branko (Jozo)	01.11.67
Barbir, Lovro (Ivan)	01.11.35
Baričević, Željko (Stjepan)	17.08.65
Barišić, Franjo (Andrija)	28.05.46
Barta, Anđelko (Ivan)	31.01.67
Batarelo, Josip (Danijel)	12.03.47
Batarelo, Željko (Ante)	25.10.55
Baumgertner, Tomislav (Tomislav)	27.11.73
Begčević, Marko (Ivo)	01.04.68
Begov, Željko (Mato)	30.09.58
Bingula, Stjepan (Stjepan)	15.10.58
Bjelanović, Ringo (Nikola)	24.11.70
Blašković, Miroslav (Mijo)	06.04.59
Blažević, Zlatko (Zdenko)	24.02.64
Bodrožić, Ante (Marijan)	07.06.53

Bosak, Marko (Juraj)	02.07.67
Bosanac, Dragutin (Lavoslav)	21.08.19
Bosanac, Tomislav (Antun)	05.03.41
Bošnjakov, Josip (Ilija)	05.09.60
Božak, Ivan (Franjo)	28.08.58
Bračić, Zvonimir (Ivan)	04.07.70
Bradarić, Josip (Šime)	02.03.49
Brajdić, Josip (Pavo)	16.03.50
Buovac, Ivan (Ilija)	03.09.66
Bužić, Zvonko (Stjepan)	27.08.55
Crnjac, Ivan (Slavko)	18.05.66
Čaleta, Zvonimir (Nikola)	24.02.53
Čolak, Ivica (Blago)	26.09.65
Čupić, Mladen (Marko)	19.05.67
Dalić, Tihomir (Zvonko)	02.11.66
Dolišni, Ivica (Petar)	27.11.60
Došen, Ivan (Ivan)	04.01.58
Došen, Martin (Ivan)	19.02.52
Došen, Tadija (Ivan)	09.10.50
Dragun, Josip (Srećko)	09.09.62
Duvnjak, Stanko (Vladimir)	23.05.59
Đuđar, Saša (Đuro)	05.03.68
Đukić, Perica	23.09.53
Đukić, Vladimir (Ivan)	21.02.48
Ebner, Vinko-Đuro (Vinko)	07.04.61
Edelinski, Goran (Vladimir)	29.07.75
Firi, Ivan (Đuro Kulik)	01.06.15
Fituš, Karlo (Ištvan)	28.09.64
Friščić, Dragutin (Matija)	02.11.58
Furundžija, Petar (Danko)	30.11.49
Gajda, Robert (Mihajlo)	27.12.66
Galić, Milenko (Mate)	10.12.65
Galić, Vedran (Ivan)	29.05.73
Garvanović, Borislav (Ivan)	23.11.54
Gašpar, Zorislav (Dragutin)	14.03.71
Gavrić, Dragan (Pavo)	31.10.56
Glavašević, Siniša (Petar)	04.11.60
Gojani, Jozo (Ivo)	01.01.66
Golac, Krunoslav (Veljko)	06.07.59
Graf, Branislav (Vladimir)	07.09.55
Granić, Dragan (Mile)	01.01.60
Grejza, Milan (Mato)	27.06.59
Gruber, Zoran (Ilija)	05.09.69
Gudelj, Drago (Ivan)	09.09.40
Gudelj, Zdravko (Marijan)	31.01.59
Hegeduš, Tomislav (Franjo)	02.11.53
Hegedušić, Mario (Dragutin)	29.06.72
Herceg, Željko (Slavko)	20.01.62
Herman, Ivan (Dragutin)	14.05.69
Herman, Stjepan (Antun)	10.03.55
Hincak, Zvonimir (Đuro)	08.09.55

165

Hlevnjak, Nedeljko (Anđelko)	08.01.64
Holjevac, Nikica (Ivan)	10.04.55
Horvat, Ivica (Josip)	27.11.58
Horvat, Viktor (Šimun)	27.08.49
Husnjak, Nedjeljko (Juraj)	30.06.69
Ileš, Zvonko (Ivan)	12.12.41
Imbrišić, Ivica (Pavle)	13.02.58
Ivan, Zlatko (Eugen)	25.12.55
Ivezić, Aleksander (Ivan)	05.12.50
Jajalo, Marko (Ivan)	28.10.57
Jakubovski, Martin (Ivan)	01.04.71
Jalšovec, Ljubomir (Antun)	02.11.57
Jambor, Tomo (Dragutin)	03.03.66
Janić, Mihael (Antun)	09.10.39
Janjić, Borislav (Ivan)	08.09.56
Jantol, Boris (Đuro)	21.09.59
Jarabek, Zlatko (Kamilo)	21.04.56
Jezidžić, Ivica (Stipo)	05.11.57
Jovan, Zvonimir (Vlatko)	07.04.67
Jovanović, Branko (Todor)	04.02.55
Jovanović, Oliver (Đuro)	08.12.72
Jularić, Goran (Andrija)	15.02.71
Jurela, Damir (Tomislav)	25.04.69
Jurela, Željko (Božo)	30.06.56
Jurendić, Drago (Juro)	23.04.66
Jurišić, Marko (Franjo)	17.08.46
Jurišić, Pavao (Pavo)	28.08.66
Jurišić, Željko (Rude)	20.12.63
Kačić, Igor (Petar)	23.08.75
Kapustić, Josip (Josip)	08.12.65
Kelava, Krešimir (Antun)	17.01.53
Kiralj, Damir (Josip)	10.03.64
Kiralj, Damir (Julije)	17.07.59
Kitić, Goran (Mitar)	23.02.66
Knežić, Đuro (Franjo)	02.04.37
Kolak, Tomislav (Dobroslav)	22.07.62
Kolak, Vladimir (Dobroslav)	20.01.66
Kologranić, Duško (Josip)	23.10.50
Komorski, Ivan (Pero)	23.06.52
Kostenac, Bono (Andrija)	15.02.42
Kostović, Borislav (Ante)	24.12.62
Košir, Božidar (Mirko)	28.09.57
Kovač, Ivan (Mate)	18.06.53
Kovač, Mladen (Branko)	20.08.58
Kovačević, Zoran (Zlata)	16.04.62
Kovačić, Damir (Tomo)	14.07.70
Kožul, Josip (Frano)	08.03.68
Krajinović, Ivan (Luka)	14.10.66
Krajinović, Zlatko (Ante)	04.12.69
Krasić, Ivan (Petar)	18.06.64
Krezo, Ivica (Hrvoje)	10.09.63

Krističević, Kazimir (Branko)	13.06.59
Križan, Drago (Jozo)	05.11.57
Kruneš, Branimir (Mate)	28.02.66
Lenđel, Tomislav (Franjo)	06.08.57
Lenđel, Zlatko (Franjo)	18.00.49
Lerotić, Zvonimir (Filip)	13.09.60
Lesić, Tomislav (Branko)	10.05.50
Let, Mihajlo (Đuro)	25.04.56
Lili, Dragutin (Dragutin)	26.01.51
Ljubas, Hrvoje (Luka)	26.01.71
Lončar, Tihomir (Đorđe)	28.03.55
Lovrić, Joko (Ivo)	06.11.68
Lovrić, Jozo (Lovro)	15.07.53
Lucić, Marko (Mijo)	08.09.54
Lukenda, Branko (Ivan)	14.04.61
Lukić, Mato (Marko)	02.03.63
Magdić, Mile (Ivan)	25.03.53
Magoč, Predrag (Mihael)	18.12.65
Majić, Robert (Tvrtko)	23.02.71
Major, Željko (Stjepan)	14.12.60
Mandić, Marko (Antun)	26.07.53
Maričić, Zdenko (Marko)	27.09.56
Marijanović, Martin (Marko)	17.08.59
Mažar, Ivan (Antun)	20.11.34
Međeši, Andrija (Janko)	16.10.36
Međeši, Zoran (Andrija)	09.09.40
Merić, Ohran (Muhamed)	10.07.56
Mihović, Tomislav (Gašpar)	23.06.52
Mikletić, Josip (Stjepan)	26.02.52
Mikulić, Zdravko (Slavko)	15.03.61
Mikulić, Zvonko (Slavko)	11.05.69
Milić, Slavko (Mijo)	17.04.55
Miljak, Zvonimir (Ivan)	10.05.50
Mišić, Ivan (Marko)	22.12.68
Mlinarić, Mile (Pavo)	05.12.66
Mokoš, Andrija (Stevan)	16.11.55
Molnar, Aleksandar (Stjepan)	08.04.65
Mutvar, Antun (Antun)	30.01.69
Nađ, Darko (Vladimir)	27.02.65
Nađ, Franjo (Franjo)	17.08.35
Nejašmić, Ivan (Milan)	19.10.58
Nicollier, Jean Michael	01.07.66
Omerović, Mersad (Jusuf)	01.01.70
Oreški, Ivan (Dragutin)	12.04.50
Papp, Tomislav (Andrija)	01.01.63
Patarić, Željko (Nikola)	16.07.59
Pavlić, Slobodan (Adam)	24.09.65
Pavlović, Zlatko (Đuro)	19.11.63
Perak, Mato (Ante)	28.11.61
Perko, Aleksandar (Branko)	17.03.67
Perković, Damir (Josip)	28.10.65

167

Perković, Josip (Jure)	24.03.63
Petrović, Stjepan (Stanko)	26.10.49
Pinter, Nikola (Nikola)	04.10.40
Plavšić, Ivan (Mato)	24.03.39
Podhorski, Janja (Stjepan)	17.11.31
Polhert, Damir (Ivan)	22.11.62
Polovina, Branimir (Vojin)	22.06.50
Posavec, Stanko (Gustav)	09.04.52
Pravdić, Tomo (Pero)	11.01.34
Prpić, Tomislav (Milan)	03.04.59
Pucar, Dmitar (Nikola)	18.01.49
Raguž, Ivan (Antun)	22.04.55
Rašić, Milan (Franjo)	16.04.54
Ratković, Krešimir (Milan)	04.03.68
Ražić, Josip	17.11.69
Ribičić, Marko (Ivan)	11.11.51
Rimac, Salvador (Slavko)	06.11.60
Rohaček, Karlo (Antun)	21.10.42
Rohaček, Željko (Karlo)	16.05.71
Saiti, Ćeman (Azem)	17.09.60
Samardžić, Damjan (Marko)	23.07.46
Savanović, Tihomir (Dragoslav)	17.07.64
Senčić, Ivan (Martin)	21.02.64
Sotinac, Stipan (Jozo)	25.11.39
Spudić, Pavao (Ivan)	17.07.65
Stanić, Marko (Mato)	02.08.58
Stanić, Željko (Niko)	23.06.68
Stefanko, Petar (Vasilije)	05.05.42
Stojanović, Ivan (Živko)	19.03.49
Stubičar, Ljubomir (Vladimir)	12.07.54
Šajtović, Davor (Martin)	13.11.61
Šajtović, Martin (Adam)	14.04.28
Šarik, Stjepan (Stefan)	02.04.55
Šaškin, Sead (Hasan)	22.03.60
Šindilj, Vjekoslav (Vladimir)	01.11.71
Šrenk, Đuro (Gabrijel)	21.04.43
Štefulj, Dražen (Juraj)	01.01.63
Tabaček, Antun (Josip)	05.06.58
Tadić, Tadija (Jozo)	26.08.59
Tarle, Dujo (Jozo)	06.05.50
Terek, Antun (Božidar)	06.10.40
Tišljarić, Darko (Tomo)	01.06.71
Tivanovac, Ivica (Pavo)	22.02.63
Tomašić, Tihomir (Albin)	04.07.63
Tordinac, Željko (Ivan)	14.12.61
Tot, Tomislav (Eugen)	06.06.67
Traljić, Tihomir (Petar)	17.07.67
Turk, Miroslav (Antun)	12.04.50
Turk, Petar (Petar)	30.06.47
Tustonjić, Dane (Jozo)	10.10.59
Tuškan, Dražen (Dragutin)	26.10.66

168

Ušak, Branko (Martin)	17.07.58
Vagenhofer, Mirko (Josip)	03.06.37
Varenica, Zvonko (Franjo)	19.05.57
Veber, Siniša (Vladimir)	22.02.69
Vidoš, Goran (Mato)	04.10.60
Vilenica, Žarko (Jovo)	19.06.69
Virges, Antun (Antun)	09.06.53
Vlaho, Mate (Drago)	03.02.59
Vlaho, Miroslav (Marko)	30.12.67
Voloder, Zlatan (Ljubo)	23.11.60
Von Basingger, Harllan (Dušan)	25.08.71
Vujević, Zlatko (Antun)	28.10.51
Vukojević, Slaven (Josip)	23.06.70
Vuković, Rudolf (Rudolf)	18.11.61
Vuković, Vladimir (Zlatko)	25.11.57
Vuković, Zdravko (Nikola)	07.09.67
Vulić, Ivan (Ante)	18.07.46
Vulić, Vid (Vid)	01.09.41
Vulić, Zvonko (Ivan)	07.06.71
Zera, Mihajlo (Vasilj)	07.08.55
Zeljko, Josip (Danko)	14.03.53
Žeravica, Dominik (Stjepan)	11.11.59
Živković, Damir (Josip)	17.11.70
Živković, Goran (Pavao)	20.12.60
Žugec, Borislav (Mato)	21.11.63

THE ACCUSED

15.   Mile MRKŠIĆ, born on 20 July 1947 near Vrginmost, Croatia, was a colonel in the JNA and was commander of the Guards Brigade which had primary responsibility for the attack on Vukovar. After the siege of Vukovar, he was promoted to general rank with the Yugoslav Army (JA) and later became the commanding officer of the Army of the "Republic of Serb Krajina."

16.   Miroslav RADIĆ, approximately 35 years of age, was a captain in the JNA. He commanded a special infantry unit which was a component of the Guards Brigade from Belgrade.

17.   Veselin ŠLJIVANČANIN, born in 1953 near Žabljak, Montenegro, was a major in the JNA in command of a military police battalion and also served as the security officer for the Guards Brigade. He was the operational commander for the JNA in the latter stages of the siege of Vukovar. Afterward, he was promoted to the rank of colonel and is now in command of a JA brigade in Podgorica, Montenegro.

GENERAL ALLEGATIONS

18.   Unless otherwise set forth below, all acts and omissions alleged in this indictment took place during November 1991 in Vukovar municipality in the Republic of Croatia in the territory of the former Yugoslavia.

169

19.   At all times relevant to this indictment, a state of international armed conflict existed in the territory of the former Yugoslavia.

20.   At all times relevant to this indictment, all persons described in this indictment as victims were protected by the Geneva Conventions of 1949.

21.   At all times relevant to this indictment, all of the accused in this indictment were required to abide by the laws and customs governing the conduct of war, including the Geneva Conventions of 1949.

22.   All acts and omissions charged as crimes against humanity were part of a widespread, systematic or large-scale attack against the non-Serb residents of the municipality of Vukovar.

23.   Each of the accused is individually responsible for the crimes alleged against him in this indictment pursuant to Article 7(1) of the Tribunal Statute. Individual criminal responsibility includes committing, planning, instigating, ordering or otherwise aiding and abetting in the planning, preparation or execution of any crimes referred to in Articles 2 to 5 of the Tribunal Statute.

24.   Each of the accused is also or alternatively criminally responsible as a commander for the acts of his subordinates pursuant to Article 7(3) of the Tribunal Statute. Command criminal responsibility is the responsibility of a superior officer for the acts of his subordinate if he knew or had reason to know that his subordinate was about to commit such acts or had done so and the superior failed to take the necessary and reasonable measures to prevent such acts or to punish the perpetrators thereof.

25.   The general allegations contained in paragraphs 18 through 24 are realleged and incorporated into each of the charges set forth below.

CHARGES

26.   On about 20 November 1991, JNA and Serb paramilitary soldiers under the command or supervision of Mile MRKŠIĆ, Miroslav RADIĆ and Veselin ŠLJIVANČANIN removed approximately 260 men from Vukovar Hospital and then transported them to a farm building in Ovčara, where they beat the men for several hours. Afterward, soldiers under the command or supervision of Mile MRKŠIĆ, Miroslav RADIĆ and Veselin ŠLJIVANČANIN transported the men in groups of 10-20 to a site between the Ovčara farm and Grabovo, where they shot and killed them. By their acts and omissions Mile MRKŠIĆ, Miroslav RADIĆ and Veselin ŠLJIVANČANIN, are criminally responsible for:

Beatings:

Count 1:   GRAVE BREACHES of the Geneva Conventions of 1949 recognised by Article 2(c) (wilfully causing great suffering) of the Tribunal Statute;

Count 2:   VIOLATIONS OF THE LAWS OR CUSTOMS OF WAR recognised by Article 3 (cruel treatment) of the Tribunal Statute;

Count 3:   CRIMES AGAINST HUMANITY recognised by Article 5(i) (inhumane acts) of the Tribunal Statute.

Killings:

Count 4:   GRAVE BREACHES of the Geneva Conventions of 1949 recognised by Article 2(a) (wilful killing) of the Tribunal Statute;

Count 5:   VIOLATIONS OF THE LAWS OR CUSTOMS OF WAR recognised by Article 3 (murder) of the Tribunal Statute;

Count 6:   CRIMES AGAINST HUMANITY recognised by Article 5(a) (murder) of the Tribunal Statute.

26 October , 1995
The Hague, The Netherlands

Richard J. Goldstone
Prosecutor

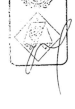

171

◆

GENOCIDE AND PROTECTION
OF CIVILIANS

The Convention on the Prevention and Punishment of the Crime of Genocide was in large part a reaction to the Nazis' systematic murder of Jews and members of certain other groups of people.

CONVENTION ON THE PREVENTION AND PUNISHMENT OF THE CRIME OF GENOCIDE

[78 U.N.T.S. 277, adopted by Resolution 260 (III) A of the General Assembly of the United Nations on December 9, 1948]

. . .

Article I. The Contracting Parties confirm that genocide, whether committed in time of peace or in time of war, is a crime under international law which they undertake to prevent and to punish.

Article II. In the present Convention, genocide means any of the following acts committed with intent to destroy, in whole or in part, a national, ethnical, racial or religious group, as such:

(a) Killing members of the group;

(b) Causing serious bodily or mental harm to members of the group;

(c) Deliberately inflicting on the group conditions of life calculated to bring about its physical destruction in whole or in part;

(d) Imposing measures intended to prevent births within the group;

(e) Forcibly transferring children of the group to another group.

Article III. The following acts shall be punishable:

(a) Genocide;

(b) Conspiracy to commit genocide;

(c) Direct and public incitement to commit genocide;

(d) Attempt to commit genocide;

(e) Complicity in genocide.

Article IV. Persons committing genocide or any of the other acts enumerated in article III shall be punished, whether they are constitutionally responsible rulers, public officials or private individuals.

Article V. The Contracting Parties undertake to enact, in accordance with their respective Constitutions, the necessary legislation to give effect to the provisions of the present Convention and, in particular, to provide effective penalties for persons guilty of genocide or of any of the other acts enumerated in article III.

Article VI. Persons charged with genocide or any of the other acts enumerated in article III shall be tried by a competent tribunal of the State in the territory of which the act was committed, or by such international penal tribunal as may have jurisdiction with respect to those Contracting Parties which shall have accepted its jurisdiction.

Article VII. Genocide and the other acts enumerated in article III shall not be considered as political crimes for the purpose of extradition.

The Contracting Parties pledge themselves in such cases to grant extradition in accordance with their laws and treaties in force.

Article VIII. Any Contracting Party may call upon the competent organs of the United Nations to take such action under the Charter of the United Nations as they consider appropriate for the prevention and suppression of acts of genocide or any of the other acts enumerated in article III.

Article IX. Disputes between the Contracting Parties relating to the interpretation, application or fulfilment of the present Convention, including those relating to the responsibility of a State for genocide or for any of the other acts enumerated in article III, shall be submitted to the International Court of Justice at the request of any of the parties to the dispute.

.   .   .

173

Appendix G

Courtesy of Institute of Public Health of the
Republic and the Federation of Bosnia and Herzegovina, Sarajevo 1996.

<table>
<tr><td>5. MEDICINSKO OSOBLJE
UBIJENO U RATU</td><td>5. KILLED MEDICAL STAFF
DURING THE WAR</td></tr>
</table>

Na narednim stranicama dat je prikaz ljekara i medicinskog osoblja regije Sarajevo nastradalih u toku bestijalne agresije na Republiku Bosnu i Hercegovinu.
Podaci nisu kompletni, jer iz objektivnih razloga nisu bile dostupne sve informacije o poginulim.

On the following pages there are physitians and members of nursing staff of the Sarajevo region killed during the bestical aggression against the Republic of Bosnia and Herzegovina.

Data are incomplete as all information on the killed has not been available for objektive reasons.

1. SUADA DILBEROVIĆ
(24 May 1968 - 5 April 1992)

apsolvent medicine

Sarajevo, predvečerje 5 april. Antiratne manifestacije na mostu Vrbanja u Sarajevu. Među prvima je i mlada Dubrovčanka, apsolvent medicine. Želi mir, želi da završi studij i radi svoj humani poziv. Ne može da shvati da to neko ne želi. Pucnji! Suadina zvjezda se gasi. Sjećanja na nju nikada.

Sarajevo, the twighlight of April 5th. Antiwar rallies on Vrbanja Bridge in Sarajevo. Among the first ones to join was a young girl from Dubrovnik, a medical degree-exam candidate. She wanted peace, she wanted to complete her studies of medicine and do her humane job. She could not understand that somebody did not wish it. Shots echoed. Suada's star fell. Memories of her will never fade.

174

2. ANTO KOZINA

(2 August 1938 - 24 April 1992)

medicinski tehničar - medical technician

Radnik Zavoda za hitnu medicinsku pomoć. Poginuo u sanitetskim kolima u pratnji pacijenta u Dobrinji od metaka u rafalno izrešetanom vozilu iz agresorske zasjede.

Worker of the Institute for Emergency Medical Aid. Killed by a bullet in the ambulance riddled with bullets from the aggressor's ambush while accompanying a patient at Dobrinja.

3. Prim. dr SILVA RIZVANBEGOVIĆ

(25 October 1948 - 17 May 1992)

spec.urgentne medicine - spec. in emergency medicine

Maja 1992 godine, snajperski hitac odnio je život dr Silve Rizvanbegović, za uvijek. Provela je četrdeset dana u ratu. Ona je ugradila svu sebe, svo svoje znanje, entuzijazam i hrabrost u ovaj humani poziv. Neumorno je hitala svojim pacijentima. Na takvom jednom putu iz ˏagresorske zasjede pucano je na sanitetsko vozilo. Otišla je Silva. Neka joj je vječna slava. Iza nje su ostali sin i kćerka.

In May 1992, a sniper's shot took away the life of Dr Silva Rizvanbegović. She worked for 40 days in this war. She completely dedicated herself, her knowledge, enthusiasm and courage to this humane profession. She tirelessly rushed to help her patients. On such a round of hers, the ambulance she was in was shot at from the aggressor's ambush. Silva passed away. Glorious may she be. She left a son and a daughter.

175

4. Dr GORDANA ČEKLIĆ

(11 January 1964 - 28 May 1992)

specijalizant iz interne medicine - resident specializing in internal medicine

Njen kratak životni vijek bio je ispunje marljivim radom. U roku je diplomirala na Medicinskom fakultetu u Sarajevu, potom stažirala i započela specijalistički staž iz interne medicine. Smrt ju je zatekla u hodu, na putu ka poslu. Bila je žrtva nečuvenog masakra u ulici Vase Miskina.

Her short lifespan was filled with diligent work. She graduated Medical Faculty in Sarajevo, then did her internship and started her residentship in internal medicine. She got killed afoot, on her way to work. She was one of the victims of the massacre unheard of, in Vase Miskina Street.

5. Dr JUSUF AHMEDSPAHIĆ

(2 October 1952 - 10 June 1992)

spec. neurohirurg - neurosurgeon

Rođen u Višegradu. Osnovnu školu i gimnaziju završio u Višegradu. Studirao u Sarajevu, gdje je i diplomirao. Po završenom studiju radio u Hitnoj medicinskoj pomoći. 1982 godine počinje specijalistički staž na Neurohirurškoj klinici u Sarajevu. Njegova velika ljubav bila je vaskularna hirurgija. Po završetku specijalizacije, upisuje postdiplomski studij. Njegov magistarski rad ostao je nedovršen. Objavljivao niz stručnih radova u domaćim i stranim časopisima. Subspecijalizaciju završio u Ljubljani. Poginuo je 10.16.1992 godine, pogođen gelerima agresorske granate. Iza njega ostala žena i dvoje maloljetne djece

He was born in Višegrad. He completed primary and secondary schools in his birthplace. He studied in Sarajevo where he graduated from the Faculty of Medicine. After taking his degree, he worked in the First Aid Centre. In 1982, he started his residentship at the Clinic for Neurosurgery in Sarajevo. Pride of his job was vascular surgery. On completing the residentship, he took postgraduate courses. His published a number of papers in national and international journals. He also completed subspecialization in Ljubljana. On June 10 1992, he was shot dead by an agressor's shell shrapnel. He left a wife and two underage children.

6.Dr GORDANA VARUNEK-VUJOVIĆ

(29 April 1949 - 24 June 1992)

spec. pedijatar - paediatrician

Diplomirala na Medicinskom fakultetu u Sarajevu. Specijalizirala pedijatriju. Bila je ljekar u dispanzerskom centru "Kumrovec" gdje ju je zatekao rat. Dana 24.06.1992 godine smrtno nastradala, pogođena snajperskim hicem, u autobusu koji je prevozio medicinske radnike, u periodu dok je grad žestoko granatiran sa okolnih brda.

Graduated from the Medical Faculty in Sarajevo. She specialized in paediatrics. She worked as a doctor at the Dispensary Centre "Kumrovec", where she still worked when the war broke out. On June 24 1992, she received a deadly wound from a sniper while riding on the bus transporting the medical workers in the period the City was heavily shelled from the surrounding hills.

7. Dr ABDURAHMAN FILIPOVIĆ

(27 November 1957 - 5 August 1992)

ljekar primarne zdravstvene zaštite - primary health care physician

Rođen u Kalinoviku kraj Sarajeva. Studij medicine završava u Sarajevu 9.07.1987. godine. Radni vijek započinje u D.Z. "Kalinovik", gdje ga zatiče i rat. Dana 1.07.1992 godine biva zarobljen i provodi zadnje dane u četničkom zatvoru u selu Jelašca kod Kalinovika. Zvjerski je likvidiran dana 5.08.1992. u zaseoku Ratine kod Jeleča skupa sa 21 licem muslimanske nacionalnosti.

Born at Kalinovik near Sarajevo, graduated from the Medical Faculty in Sarajevo on July 9 1987. He started his career at the Health Centre "Kalinovik" where he still was when the war broke out. On June 30 or July 1 1992, he was captured and put to a chetnik prison in the village of Jelešca near Kalinovik. On August 5 1992 he was brutally killed in the hamlet of Ratine near Jeleč along with 21 other persons of Muslim ethic affiliation. .

177

8. ARFAN OPIJAĆ

(9 July 1945 - 23 August 1992)

medicinski tehničar - medical technician

Medicinski tehničar Zavoda za hitnu medicinsku pomoć. Ubijen 23.08.1992. godine od gelera granate dok je išao u kućnu posjetu pacijentu.

Worked as a medical technician in the Institute for Emergency Medical Aid. Killed on August 23 1992 by a shrapnel while on a round to see a patient.

9. HARIS MERZIĆ

(19 July 1965 - end of 1992)

apsolvent medicine - medical degree-exam candidate

Tačan datum njegove smrti se ne zna. Kao još nezavršeni ljekar, obavljao svoj posao do četničkog napada na sarajevsko naselje Otes. gdje su ga zarobili, a potom zlikovački likvidirali.

Exact date of his death is unknown. As an undergraduate medical student, he practised medicine until the chetniks attacked the Sarajevo settlement of Otes. He was caputured there and later perfidiously killed.

10. Dr MUSTAFA PINTOL

(15 May 1964 - end of 1992)

ljekar primarne zdravstvene zaštite - primary health care physician

Rođen u Lukavcu, opština Trnovo. U odsutnim bitkama za odbranu grada i mlade države nesebično je obavljao svoj posao. Smrt ga je zatekla na jednom od mnogih radnih zadataka. Snajperski hitac odveo ga je u vječnost.

Born at Lukavac, the municipality of Trnovo. In the crucial battles for the defence of the City and young state, he unselfishly did his duty of a physician. He got killed while attending to one of his many duties. A sniper's bullet took him to eternity.

11. MUNIRA SULJEVIĆ

(- 5 December 1992)

medicinska sestra - nurse

Radila kao medicinska sestra na Psihijatrijskoj klinici. Poginula na radnom mjestu 5.12.1992 godine kao još jedna žrtva strašne agresije.

She worked as a nurse at the Psychiatric Clinic. She got killed at her workplace on December 5 1992, as another victim of this terrible aggression.

179

12. ADMIR JELEŠKOVIĆ

(29 June 1969 - 6 January 1993)

medicinski tehničar - medical technician

Poginuo na putu prema radnom mjestu dana 6.01.1993. godine. Bio uposlen kao medicinski tehničar na Psihijatrijskoj klinici - Sarajevo.

Killed on his way to work on January 6 1993. He worked as a medical technician at the Psychiatric Clinic Sarajevo.

13. Dr VLADO BILJENKI

(9 March 1934 - 30 January 1993)

spec. oftalmolog - ophthalmologist

Radni i životni vijek proveo u Sarajevu i utkao u Očnu kliniku, gdje je bio šef odjeljenja. Krasile su ga sve vrline ljekara humaniste i ljudska dobrota. Iako krhkog zdravlja od početka agresije neumorno radio. Smrt ga je sustigla pred operacionom salom 30.01.1993. godine. Usmrćen je gelerom agresorske granate. Za njim ostala supruga, sin i kćerka.

He worked and lived in Sarajevo all his life dedicationg himself to the Ophthalmological Clinic where he was the Ward head. He possessed the kindness of a humanist doctor. Although his health was frail, he worked tirelessly from the very beginning of the agression. He was shot dead by a shrapnel just outside the operating theatre on January 30 1993. He left a wife. a son and a daughter.

14. Dr SEMIR ARIFHODŽIĆ

(22 August 1961 - 4 June 1993)

ljekar primarne zdravstvene zaštite - primary health care physician

Svi koji su poznavali dr Arifhodžića sjećaju se blage fizionomije i vječnog osmjeha. Izuzetno vrijedan, započeo je svoj rad u medicini upisom na Medicinski fakultet 1981 godine. Diplomirao je u roku. Prolazi kroz sve teške napade na Sarajevo. Jedna agresorska granata prekida nemilosrdno ovaj radni životni vijek.

All those who remember Dr Arifhodžić remember his mild smiling face. Exceptionally hard-working, he started his engagement in medical profession by enrolling in the Medical Faculty in 1981. He graduated in strictly fixed term of studies. He went through all the attacks on Sarajevo before a shell mercilessly endedhis work and life.

15. Prim. dr RAMIZ KOMILIJA

(8 March 1936 - 5 August 1993)

spec.ginekolog akušer -obstetrician - gynaecologist

Prije rata radio u mjestu Hadžići kraj Sarajeva. Po početku agresije nastavio obavljati dužnosti u Zavodu za zaštitu žene i materinstva Sarajevo. Dana 16.02.1993 godine teško ranjen snajperskim hicem sa Grbavice, pred samim ulazom u zgradu Hitne pomoći. U teškom stanju proveo šest mjeseci. Njegovo srce nije izdržao. Preminuo je 5.08.1993.godine. Za njim je ostala supruga i pet kćeri.

Before the war, he worked at Hadžići, a small town near Sarajevo. When the war broke out, he continued his practice in the Institute for the Protection of Women and Motherhood in Sarajevo. On February 16 1993, he was badly wounded at the very entrance to the First Aid building by a sniper's bullet that was fired from Grbavica. In a very bad condition, he spent six months. His heart failed. He passed away on August 5 1993. He left a wife and five daughters.

181

16. Prim.dr GALIB PLEHO

(31 March 1931 - 9 December 1993)

ljekar primarne zdravstvene zaštite - primary health care physician

Rat ga je zatekao u pedijatrijskoj službi Doma zdravlja "Novi Grad", čiji je direktor uskoro postao. Funkciju direktora Doma zdravlja obavljao je u najtež em periodu sarajevske drame. Tu ga je sustigla smrt. Stradao je od agresorske granate, u trenutku vršenja radne dužnosti, u neposrednoj blizini DZ "Novi Grad". Za njim je ostala supruga i dva sina studenta.

When the war broke out, he worked in the paediatric ward of the Health Centre "Novi Grad", whose director he was soon to become. He exercised the function of doctor in the most critical period of the Sarajevo drama. It is there that he died. He was killed by a shell while on duty, in the immediate vicinity of H.C. "Novi Grad". He left a wife and two sons university students.

17. IGOR PAVLOVIĆ

(2 December 1969 - 24 December 1993)

apsolvent medicine - medical degree-exam candidate

Rat mu je prekinuo najljepše šetnje. I ljubavi i radosti. Ostao je u rodnom gradu. Našao je nove šetnje radosti i ljubavi. Na njegovoj počasnoj diplomi, koja je posmrtno dodjeljena, stoji:

"Imao si dvije ljubavi iznad svega - medicinu i domovinu. Izabrao si ovu drugu i za nju dao mladi život, da bi Tvoje kolege mogle studirati."

The war interrupted his most beautiful walks. His loves and his joys, too. He stayed in his home town, discovered new walks, new joys and loves. In his honorary diploma, which he was awarded posthumously, it reads:

" You had two loves above all - medicine and Your country. You chose the latter and gave Your young life for her so that Your colleagues might study."

182

18. Prim. dr ZDRAVKO BALABANOVIĆ

(1939 - 31 December 1993)
spec.ginekolog akušer - obstetrician-gynaecologist

Prim. dr Zdravko Balabanović je još jedna od žrtava bezočne agresije na Republiku Bosnu i Hercegovinu. Tih i vrijedan proveo je svoj radni i životni vijek u Sarajevu. Smrt ga je sustigla u trenutku kada se vraćao sa posla, pred samim kućnim vratima. Smrt je bila trenutna.

Prim.Dr Zdravko Balabanović is another victim of ruthless aggression against the Republic of Bosnia and Herzegovina. Quiet and diligent, he spent all his life working in Sarajevo. Death took him away while he was on his way home from work, at the very front door of his house.

19. ŠEFIKA HEČO

(- January 1994)

medicinska sestra - nurse

Medicinska sestra na Abdominalnoj hirurgiji. Smrt ju je zatekla na radnom mjestu. Usmrćena gelerom granate, onom koja je direktno gađala zgradu Abdominalne hirurgije u Sarajevu.

She worked as a nurse at the Abdominal Clinic. She also was killed at her workplace. She was killed by a shrapnel of a shell directly targeting the Abdominal Surgery building, Sarajevo.

183

20. SUADA KUPUS

(- January 1994)

medicinska sestra - nurse

Nastradala na radnom mjestu, kao žrtva bestijalnog granatiranja objekta kliničkog Centra u Sarajevu.

She was killed at her workplace as a victim of bestial shelling of a Clinical Centre building Sarajevo.

21. Dr ELIESAD KLANČEVIĆ
(30.August 1945 - 30 May 1993)
Specijalista ortodoncije - Specialist of orthodoncy

Rođen u Srebrenici 30.08.1945 . Stomatološki fakultet i specijalizaciju iy ortodoncije završio je u Sarajevu. Poginuo je na aerodromskoj pisti u Sarajevu prilikom povratka mobilne ekipe iy Goražda ya Sarajevo 30.05.1993.godine. Iya dr Eliesada Klančevića ostalaje supruga.

Born in Srebrenica on 30 August 1945. He graduated from the Stomatological Faculty and completed his specialization in Sarajevo.Killed on the airplane ronway in Sarajevo while the mobile teamwas coming bade from Goražde to Sarajevo on 30 May 1993. Dr Eliesad Klančević left a wife.

184

22. Dr AZIZ TORLAK
(1950 - nestao 1993)
(1950 - missing from 1993)

Specijalista opšte hirurgije - Specijalist of general surgery Rođen 1950 godine u selu Lase, opština Rogatica Osnovnu školu završio u Rogatici. Srednju medicinsku školu završio u Foči. Medicinski fakultet završio u Sarajevu. Radio kao ljekar opšte medicine u Rogatici. Nakon specijalizacije iy opšte hirurgije, koju je završio u Sarajevu, radio u Foči kao hirurg. Poslije pada Foče zatvoren jeu zatvoru u Foči i do juna 1993 godine bio je živ. Dobio je dozvolu da izađe. Na starom mostu na Drini u Foči je izveden na razmjenu. Od tada mu se gubisvaki trag. Iza njega je ostala supruga i dvije kćeri.

He was born in 1950 in the Laze vilage, Rogatica community. Primary school hecompleted in Rotatica. Secondary medical school he completed in Sarajevo. He worked as a general practicioner in Rogatica. After finishing his specialization of general surgery in Sarajevo, he worked as surgeon in Foča. After occupation of Foča he wastaken to the prison in Foča and untill June 1993 he was alive. He got the permission to go out. He was taken for the exchange on the oldbridge on the river Drina in Foča. From that moment any trail of him has been lost. He left a wife and two daughters.

23. Dr ASIM SADIKOVIĆ
(1926 - 19.September 1993)
Specijalista medicine rada - Specialistof medicine of work

Rođen je u Ljubuškom 1926 godine. Osnovnu školu i gimnaziju završio jeu Trebinju i Mostaru. Medicinski fakultet završio je u Sarajevu 1955 godine. Radio jekao ljekar u Ljubuškom, Sarajevu i Mostaru. Tragi;no jepreminuo u Mostaru 19.09.1993. godine. Sahranjen je u Ljubuškom. Iyanjega je ostala supruga. Ostaoje u lijepom sjećanju mnogih pacijenata zbog svoje dobrote i humanosti.

He was born in Ljubuški in 1926. Primary school and Gymnasium he completed in Trebinje and Mostar.He graduatedfrom the Medical Faculty in Sarajevo in 1955. He workedas a medical doctor in Ljubuški, Sarajevo and Mcstar. He died tragically in Mostar on 19th September 1993. He was buvialed in Ljubuški. He left a wife. He remained in nice memory of many patients because of his goodness and humanity.

185

24. DR HUSEIN HALILOVIĆ
(5.January 1958 - 7 May 1995)
Specijalista pedijatrije -Pediatriciau

Rođen je 05.01.1958 godine u Srebrenici. Srednju školu završio je u Sarajevu. Diplomirao je na Medicinskom fakultetu u Sarajevu 1982.godine. Specijaliyaciju iy pedijatrije završio u Sarajevu.

Poginuo je vršeći svoju ljekarsku dužnost na povratku iy Tuzle u Srebrenicu 07.05.1995. godine

He was boru on 5th January 1958 in Srebrenica. Secondary school he completed in Sarajevo. He graduated from the Medical Faculty in Sarajevo in 1982. Specialization of pediatrics he completed in Sarajevo. He was killed while performing his medical duty on his way back from Tuzla to Srebrenica on 7 May 1995.

25. Dr IRFAN LJUBIJANKIĆ
(26 November 1952 - 28 May 1995)

Specijalista ORL - ORL specialist

Ministar vanjskih poslova Republike/Federacije Bosne i Hercegovine rođen je u Bihaću 26. novembra 1952. godine. Osnovno i srednje obrazovanje završio je u Bihaću 1971. godine. Medicinski fakultet je završio u Beogradu 1977. godine. Specijalizirao je otorinolaringologiju u Zagrebu od 1980-1984. godine. Magistriraoje 1984. godine iy oblasti maksilofacijalne hirurgije. Iste godine je bio šef odjeljenja ya ORL regionalne bolnice u Bihaću. Pored medicine bavio se muzikom i pisao poeziju a poznavao je više stranih jezika. 1992. godine izabran je za

Minister of external affairs of Republic/Federation of Bosnia-Herzegovina was born on 26 November 1952 in Bihać and he completed secondary school in 1971 in Bihać. He graduated from the Medical Faculty in Belgrade in 1977. He was specializing otorinolaringology in Zagreb from 1980-1984. He completed his master exam of maxilofacial surgery in 1984. He was the head of ORL department of the Regional hospital in Bihać during the same year. Beside medicine he was occupied by the music and he was writing a poety, and he spoke several world languages. In 1992 he was choosen for the president

186

predsjednika opštine Bihać. Od iste godine je ;lan Centralnog i IzvrŠnog odbora SDA. Ministar vanjskih poslova R/FBiH postao je 1.11.1993. godine. Predsjednik Glavnog odbora SDA postao je 1994. godine.

Smrtno jestradao28.05.1995. godine u helikopteru obavljajući radni zadatak. Iza njega je ostala supruga i dvoje djece.

of Bihać community. From that year he was a member of the Central and Execitive committee of Moslem party SDA. He became Minister of external affairs of R/F of B-H on 1 November 1993. He became the president of the leading committee of SDA in 1994. He was killed on 28 May 1995 in the helicopter while performing his working talk. He left a wife and two children.

26. Prim. Dr MENSUR ŠABULIĆ

(16 November 1942 - 28 May 1995)
Specijalista ginekologije - Gynaecologist

Rođen je 16.11.1942. godine u Bihaću. Osnovnu školu i gimnaziju završio u Bihaću 1960. godine, kada se upisao na Medicinski fakultet u Zagrebu. Istije završio u februaru 1967 godine odkada je počeo raditi u Općoj bolnici Bihać. Specijalizaciju iz ginekologije završio 1973. godiňe, a 1978. godine dobio zvanje primarijusa. 1979.godine izabran je za direktora Regionalne bolnice u Bihaću. Od septembra 1993.godine, po odluci Skupštine okruga Bihać i Komande 5.Korpusa Armije BiH obavlja dužnost u Zagrebu. Smrtno stradao na radnom zadatku sa dr Irfanom Ljubljankićem 28.05.1995.godine.

He was born on 16 th November 1942 in Bihać. Primary school and Gymnasionhe completed in Bihać in 1960 when he entered the Medical Faculty in Zagreb. He graduated from that Faculty in February 1967 from when he started to work in the General hospital in Bihać. He finished his specialization of gynaecology in 1973, and in 1978 he got the primarius title. In 1979 he was choosen for the Head of the Regional hospital in Bihać. From September 1993 according to the decision of Parlament of district of Bihać and Command of the fifth Corps of Army of B-H, he performed his duty in Zagreb. He was killed on his working tas kwith Dr Irfan Ljubijankić on 5th May 1995.

187

Na osnovu do sada prikupljenih podataka, dajemo imena ljekara i medicinskog osoblja koji su poginuli i nestali širom Bosne i Hercegovine.

According to the up to now collected data, these are names of medical workers killed and missed all over Bosnia and Herzegovina.

27. Dr SALAHUDIN VIŠEGRAĐANIN

spec.opšte medicine - specialist of general medicine

Sarajevo

28. Dr SEAD ŠEBIĆ

spec.otorinolaringolog - ENT

Sarajevo

29. Dr ASIM HRAPOVIĆ

spec.interne medicine - internist

Sarajevo

30. Dr JELICA HADŽIHASANOVIĆ

spec.medicine rada - labour medicine

Hrasnica - Sarajevo

31. MARSELA GAVRANKAPETANOVIĆ

farmaceut - pharmacist

Sarajevo

32. Dr MEHMED HUSEINEFENDIĆ

Tuzla

33. Dr SALKO ŠAHMANOVIĆ

Vlasenica

34. Dr NIJAZ DŽANIĆ
Srebrenica

35. Dr HAMDIJA HALILOVIĆ
Srebrenica

36. Dr AVDO BAKaLOVIĆ
(nestao - missing)
Srebrenica

37. Dr NASER SIRUČIĆ
(nestao - missing)
Srebrenica

38. Dr BEĆO ČEHIĆ
Bihać

39. Dr NAZIFA OMERAGIĆ
Gradažac

40. NENAD JURIĆ
farmaceut - pharmacist
Goražde

41. BEHRUDIN KARAVDIĆ
farmaceut - pharmacist
Goražde

189

42. DUŠANKA VUJASIĆ

stomatolog - dentist

Goražde

43. Dr HASAN IMAMOVIĆ

spec.ortodont - orthodontist

Goražde

44. Dr ALMIRA ČAMDŽIĆ

Mostar

45. ŠEVALA HODžIĆ
medicinska sestra - nurse
Sarajevo

46. AZRA LAĆEVIĆ
stomatološka sestra -nurse
Sarajevo

47. Dr SUAD HASANBEGOVIĆ
stomatolog - stomatologist
Kalnovik

48. Dr MUHAREM DELJKOVIĆ
specijalista pneumoftiyiologije-pneumophtisiologist
Srebrenica

49. SELVER AMIDŽIĆ
medicinski tehničar - medical technician
Konjic

50. ADMIRA MUHAREMOVIĆ
medicinska sestra - nurse
Brčko

51. NEDŽAD MUSIĆ
viši medicinski tehničar - higher medical technician
Sarajevo

52. ASNAN DOMACIĆ
viši medicinski tehničar - higher medical technician

53. RAJKO HRKAČ
viši medicinski tehničar - higher medicaltechnician
Široki Brijeg

54. MEVLIDA PRELJEVIĆ
medicinska sestra - nurse
Sarajevo

55. Dr ESAD SADIKOVIĆ
specijalista otorinolaringolog - otorinolaringologist
Logor Omarska - Omarska prisoner of war camp
Regija Bihać

56. Dr JUSUF PAŠIĆ
Logor Omarska - Omarska prisoner of war camp Regija Bihać

57. Dr OSMAN MAHMULJIN
specijalista internista - specialist of internal medicine
Logor Omarska - Omarska prisoner of war camp
Regija Bihać

58. Dr ŽELJKO SIKALO
stomatolog - stomatologist
Logor Omarska - Omarska prisoner of war camp
Regija Bihać

59. Dr RUFAD SULJANOVIĆ
Logor Omarska - Omarska prisoner of war camp
Regija Bihać

60. Dr MEHMED SULJANOVIĆ
Logor Omarska -Omarska prisoner of war camp
Regija Bihać

191

61. Dr ENES BEGIĆ
Logor Omarska - Omarska prisoner of war camp
Regija Bihać

62. SHEHAB KHALID MOHAMED
student treće godine medicine - student of the third year of medicine

63. Dr SEAD HALILOVIĆ
Regija Bihać

64. SULEJMAN PILAV
medicinski tehničar - medical technician
Regija Bihać

65. BAHRIJA ALIĆ
medicinska sestra - nurse
Regija Bihać

66. MUJESIRA IMŠIREVIĆ
medicinska sestra - nurse
Regija Bihać

67. LUTVO MEHMEDOVIĆ
(nestao - missing)
laborant - laboratory technician
Regija Bihać

68. HASAN SMAJIĆ
(nestao - missing)
laborant - laboratory technician
Regija Bihać

69. ABDULSADIK VELIĆ
(nestao-missing)
Regija Bihać

70. NEHRUDIN SULEJMANOVIĆ
(nestao - missing)
medicinski tehničar - medical tecnician
Regija Bihać

71. REŠAD BEKRIĆ
(nedstao - missing)
laborant -laboratory technician
Regija Bihać

72. SENAID SALIHOVIĆ
(nestao-missing)
medicinski tehničar - medical technician
Regija Bihać

73. SADIK AHMETOVIĆ
(nestao - missing)
medicinski tehničar - medical technician
Regija Bihać

74. REDŽO BABIĆ
(nestao - missing)
medicinski tehničar - medical technician
Srebrenica

75. RAGIB MEHMEDOVIĆ
(nestao - missing)
medicinski tehničar - medical tehnician
Regija Bihać

76. NUSRET JUSUPOVIĆ
(nestao - missing)
zubni tehničar - dental tehnician
Regija Bihać

77. NASIB ŠPIONIĆ
(nestao missing)
učenik medicinske škole - pupil of School for medical technicians
Regija Bihać

78. MEHMEDALIJA DADIĆ
(nestao missing)
medicinskitehničar - medical technician
Regija Bihać

79. DRAGAN ŠOLAJA
medicinski tehni;ar - medical technician
Sarajevo

80. MIRKO BABIĆ
medicinski tehničar - medical technician
Sarajevo

81. JASMINKA DINOVIĆ
medicinska sestra - nurse
Sarajevo

82. FATIMA BEČIREVIĆ
medicinska sestra - nurse
Sarajevo

83. ASIM JUNUZOVIĆ
medicinskitehničar - medical technician
Sarajevo

84. FATIMA MEHANOVIĆ
medicinska sestra - nurse
Sarajevo

85. DŽEMAL MEHAKOVIĆ
medicinski tehničar - medical technician
Sarajevo

86. ALMASA STANOJEVIĆ
viši medicinski laborant - higher medical laboratory technician
Sarajevo

87. EDIN BRAJEVIĆ
medicinski tehni;ar - medical technician
Sarajevo

88. ISMET DURAKOVIĆ
viši medicinskitehničar - higher medical technician
Nevesinje

89. Dr ASIM SIVRO
(13 October 1956 - 16 January 1994)
Vitez

90. MUHAREM BERBIĆ
medicinski tehničar - medical technician
Zenica

91. BEĆIR HODŽIĆ
Sanitarni tehničar - sanitary technician
Zenica

92. RAMIZ DELIĆ
medicinski tehničar - medical technician
Zenica

93. ZAHID KARAMUJA
medicinski tehničar - medical technician
Zenica

94. HUSEIN HODŽIĆ
medicinski tehničar - medical technician
Zenica

95. Dr MIRSAD KADIĆ
Zenica

96. FARUK BRODARIĆ
medicinski tehničar - medical technician
Maglaj

97. Dr ABDULAH KARAHMET
specijalista dermatolog - dermatologist
Sarajevo

98. JADRANKA BLIŽNJAKOVIĆ
medicinska sestra - nurse
Zavidovići

99. FADILA MUHAREMOVIĆ
medicinska sestra - nurse
Zavidovići

195

100. ISMET LEKO
medicinski tehni;ar - medical technician
Travnik

101. MEHRUDIN RIBO
medicinski tehničar - medical technician
Travnik

102. MUHAREM BERBIĆ
medicinski tehni;ar - medical technician
Kakanj

103. MUNEVER BEĆIROVIĆ
medicinski tehničar - medical technician
Kakanj

104. Dr MIRSAD KADIĆ
Kakanj

105. BRADARIĆ FADIL
medicinski tehni;ar - medical technician
Maglaj

106. Dr ZENAID HADŽIALIĆ
Konjic

107. SALKO TABAKOVIĆ
medicinski tehni;ar - medical technician
Konjic

108. Dr MUHAMED PAŠIĆ
specijalista ginekologije i akušerstva - gynaecologist and obstetrician
Goražde

109. Dr ZAHIR KLEMPIĆ
Specijalista ortodoncije - specialist of orthodoncy
Srebrenica

110. ARIF KAJTAZIVIĆ
Regija Bihać

111. MERSUDIN MUJIĆ
Regija Bihać

112. ADNAN SARAČ
Regija Bihać

113. HASNIJA ŠEHIĆ
(19.01.1949-23.09.1992)
Medicinska sestra - nurse)
Ripač

114. MUHO ZAJKIĆ
Regija Bihać

115. ADIL KOMIĆ
(1927 - 12.07.1994)
Medicinski tehničar - medical tehnician
Pečigrad

116. ALEN MEŠIĆ
Regija Bihać

117. ADIL ALIĆ
Regija Bihać

118. SENAD BURZIĆ
Regija Bihać

119. Dr DRAGO GAĆUŠA
(14.06.1957 - 12.12.1994)
Bihać